New Edition
Study Guide Included

MW00763638

MAKING
WISE
CHOICES
IN LIFE

Boniface G. Gitau

Making Wise Choices in Life

2nd Revised Edition 2012

A Publication of: Vessel of Honor International Ministries
P.O. Box 24273
Cincinnati, OH 45224 USA
information@vesselofhonor.org
www.vesselofhonor.org

ISBN-13: 978-1477525081
ISBN-10: 1477525084

1st Edition 2009

Contents

STUDY GUIDE LESSONS

About This New Edition

We thank God for the increasing demand and positive feedback we continually receive from readers of the first edition of Making Wise Choices in Life. It has ministered to literary hundreds of people in different parts of the world. Churches, bible study groups, and even schools have found the book resourceful for gleaning wisdom for everyday living.

We are pleased to let you know that this new edition includes two new chapters, *Guard Against Deception* and *Guard Against Toxic Relationships,* which are key in guarding against making wrong choices. It also includes a study guide that is ideal for individual and group studies. The study guide lessons entail questions that are designed to provide in-depth and productive discussions on making wise choices.

It is our prayer that this book will offer you knowledge, wisdom and insight in making wise choices in life.

Acknowledgements

In the summer of 2006, I wrote an article in *Revival Springs Magazine* entitled "Making Wise Choices in Life." The response was phenomenal. To this day, I still receive emails from people who found that message to be a great influence and inspiration. Their responses inspired me to write this book. So I thank all the *Revival Springs Magazine* readers who took the time to let me know how my article ministered to them.

I appreciate the love of my life, my wife Dorcas, who has been a great encourager, motivator, and source of support throughout the entire project.

I thank God for my son, Joseph who relentlessly ran to the printer to pick up the countless number of drafts I printed.

I also praise God for my daughter, Rebecca who keeps praying, "May dad write a hundred and one books."

I thank Sharilyn Grayson for her outstanding work in proofreading and editing my manuscripts.

Much appreciation to Dr. Alex Chege for his input and detailed work in editing the study guide.

Thanks to my pastor Dr. David Bittinger, Montgomery Assemble of God; Pastor Chris Beard, Peoples Church; Dr. Dora Bronston, LINKS University; and Dr Ralph Godfrey Sr., New Life Temple, for your kind words and endorsement of this book.

Above all, I thank my LORD and Savior, Jesus Christ, who has given me the grace, insight, knowledge, and honor to write this book.

Foreword

Life is filled with many choices which direct our path each day. In this mired of choices it is important to choose those things which will bring God's blessings upon our lives and those around us. Boniface Gitau has provided in *Making Wise Choices in Life* a practical guide with biblical accuracy and application of how to make choices with godly wisdom.

He challenges us to take responsibility for our choices by confronting the poor choices of our past and seeking the Holy Spirit to help us in changing our way of thinking about those choices. His compassionate approach to a topic which affects all humans is refreshing and compelling. The study guide at the conclusion of the book provides real life insights into the lives of biblical characters from who the reader can glean much personal understanding.

The scriptural foundations provided of how to guard ones heart against damaging choices, lies of the enemy and destructive relationships provides a solid foundation upon which one can develop their skills in making healthy life choices. Gitau continually points the reader toward God as the Good Shepherd who leads us through difficult days by making Him our Counselor on our journey of life. And to find fulfillment in choosing God's good plan for your life will lead a person to make the most critical choice for life and eternity—a personal relationship with God through accepting Jesus Christ as Savior and Lord.

As a pastor, educator and church leader I highly recommend this book to individuals seeking a life of hope and happiness through learning to make wise choices according to God's eternal wisdom. May God bless you as you read this treasure of biblical practical life lessons from God's heart.

Rev. Dr. David L. Bittinger
Lead Pastor, Montgomery Assembly of God Church
Cincinnati, Ohio

Endorsements

I have known Boniface Gitau for more than five years. I first met him as a graduate student. After he received his master's degree, I saw his desire to teach. When he accepted my offer to become a professor at Solid Rock Bible College, I witnessed the passion he had to equip students for ministry.

Boniface teaches the Word of God with authority. He rightly divides the Word of truth. As he pours out his heart, he is primarily concerned that each student understands the lessons. As a gifted teacher, I am not surprised that he has written two books. In his first book, *Becoming a Vessel of Honor,* he encourages righteous living. In this book, *Making Wise Choices in Life,* he speaks of the responsibility people have to make right choices in their lives and stresses accountability to help them do so. Indeed, we are the total sum of our choices.

Sharing his wisdom, Pastor Gitau teaches many more people than just his students through his writings. God has shown me in the last few years the need for saints to write. Books can go where no man may ever set his foot. In equipping the saints, Pastor Boniface has a heart to see the body of Christ mature globally. His books are a must read. I plan to incorporate these writings as course textbooks.

Dr. Dora Bronston
President, LINK Theological University
Linton, Indiana

I feel so honored to recommend to you this carefully crafted treasure-trove of practical spiritual wisdom. Rev. Boniface G. Gitau is a faithful man whom God has given the gifts of wisdom, gentleness, and love. Through him, the LORD is giving His church quality instruction for living life free from regret and condemnation.

In *Making Wise Choices in Life*, I see a culmination of the core principles Boniface lives daily as a husband, a father, and a minister of the gospel. Each chapter of this book adds depth and texture to Scripture and gives the reader the tools to answer one of the most prevalent questions in the minds of so many Christians: "How can I know and then do God's will for my life?"

The more the church practices wise and godly decision making, the more God's kingdom will advance through healthy, fruit-bearing Christians. I pray that all who read this book will grow years spiritually in just the few days you spend meditating on the good and godly counsel in this book. I believe that *Making Wise Choices in Life* is from the LORD and that it is timely for your walk in Christ. I know that it is for mine.

> *Pastor Chris Beard*
> *Lead Pastor, Peoples Church*
> *Cincinnati, Ohio*

A few years ago, a pastor at my local church introduced me to Pastor Boniface Gitau. Through that introduction, I have found a man who has an outstanding gift for teaching and who is full of the Spirit of God. Ever since our meeting, he has become a great joy to our local body as well as a renowned inspiration in teaching at New Life Temple Bible College (NLTBC), a school of spiritual learning established in Cincinnati, Ohio.

Pastor Gitau is not only a gifted teacher but also an exceptional author. His first book, *Becoming a Vessel of*

Honor, greatly encouraged me, and I know that his second book, *Making Wise Choices in Life,* will truly inspire anyone who will grasp the importance of making right choices. Those who read the book will better understand how to make right choices. This valuable information will open your eyes to see that many times what is defeating us is not the devil but the erroneous choices we make in life. I believe that this book will edify everyone who reads it, showing them that making right choices will motivate growth and promote a lifestyle of success.

Dr. Ralph Godfrey
President, New Life Temple Bible College
Senior Pastor, New Life Temple Church
Cincinnati, Ohio

Preface

The Devil Made Me Do It

I once heard the story of a preacher who, while walking in the wilderness one day, came across some demons seated on a rock crying. Puzzled by this unusual sight, the preacher asked them, "Why are you crying?"

"Because of the Christians," said the demons.

"What did they do?" inquired the preacher.

"They blame us for things we haven't done," replied the demons.

As amusing as this fable might seem to be, could it be that sometimes we blame the devil for the wrong choices we have made in life? We should not

It is said, *Life is a sum of decisions made in the past.*

wonder that some so-called demons don't get cast out even after much prayer, fasting, and binding. The reality is that some of the consequences we face are not the result of demonic oppression but of the unwise decisions we have made. James 1:14 says, *But each one is tempted when, by his own evil desire, he is dragged away and enticed.*

The carnal side of us never wants to take responsibility for our own poor choices. We always want to blame others. And if we cannot blame another person, then we blame the devil. After all, don't we sound more spiritual when we tell others that we are dealing with spiritual warfare than when we admit our mistakes?

> *Regardless of your past, tomorrow is a clean slate. You can choose what to write on the clean slate.*
>
> Zig Ziglar

Think about it: when God confronted Adam for eating from the forbidden tree, he blamed his wife, Eve, who in turn blamed the devil. But God wants us to learn to take responsibility for our mistakes. Admitting our mistakes or unwise decisions does not mean that we are feeble Christians; if anything, confession reveals our strength. Owning up to error takes courage.

It is said, *Life is a sum of decisions made in the past.* For this reason, we must carefully and wisely decide our course, because every decision leads to a specific destiny. Unfortunately, many people who make unwise choices still expect to get pleasant results. What they forget is that making choices is like sowing seeds. At some point, whether in ten or twenty years, the choices they made will eventually bear fruit.

Thankfully, God still cherishes hope for us, even when we have made wrong choices. Although many people appear to be stuck in the rut of guilt and condemnation for their unwise choices, they do not have to live that way. God does not intend for anyone to live in the guilt of yesterday. Zig Ziglar puts it this way: _Regardless of your past, tomorrow is a clean slate. You can choose what to write on the clean slate._ Don't let the devil hold you hostage because of your past. God has planned a bright future for you. He wants to guide you into making wise choices.

I pray that this book will not just sit on your shelf as part of your spiritual book collection, but that you will actively guard yourself against making wrong choices after reading it.

I also pray that God will grant you the kind of inspiration and revelation that will change your life for His glory.

Preface _____

Chapter 1

Why People Make Wrong Choices in Life

Every day presents us with an abundance of options. We must choose between them very wisely, because the choices we make will affect our lives now, the lives of those around us, and our future lives. The world offers us good and bad choices daily; our responsibility, therefore, is to know the difference between the two. Many people make wrong choices in life because they fail to address the various influences on their decision making. To avoid making the same mistakes, we must identify these influences in order.

Ignorance

Ignorance is the condition that results when we do not have knowledge or experience in a particular area. When we have insufficient information about a matter, we cannot make a wise judgment about it. People often say, *Do not judge a book by its cover.* In the same way that we have to read an entire book in order to have enough information to form a just opinion of it, whenever we make important decisions, we must become fully informed about the possible consequences, because the decisions we make today will affect our lives tomorrow.

The Bible says, *My people are destroyed for lack of knowledge,* (Hosea 4:6). Making decisions out of ignorance may cost us more than we can pay. And being a Christian does not exempt us from the consequences of the poor choices we made out of ignorance. In any court of law, ignorance is no defense. Lawbreakers have to pay the full price of justice for laws broken in ignorance.

If you are planning to open a business, start a ministry, or get married, prayer and faith alone will not make you successful. God expects you to put your faith and prayers to work. The apostle James says that *"faith without works is dead"* (James 2:26). Research the kind of business you want to open; learn what works and what doesn't. If you don't do your homework, pretty soon you will be blaming others or the devil for your failures. If you are in a relationship, don't just pray; spend quality time building a healthy relationship that will lead to a successful marriage. At any rate, do whatever you must to be well informed (seek knowledge) before making important decisions.

> *The problem with succumbing to peer influence is that it makes you a slave to pleasing others. You never experience the freedom of being yourself and enjoying the blessings God has uniquely given to you.*

Peer Influence

Sometimes we strive unreasonably to maintain a certain social status or membership in a clique. We can base some vital decisions on what our peers are doing. Many people tend to think that this problem only afflicts teenagers. However, how many people live beyond their incomes just to mirror the latest trends? Whether you are talking about how you dress, where you live, what you eat, or what you drive, living to please others at the expense of financial health and family peace is a foolish and unfortunate choice.

The problem with succumbing to peer influence is that it makes you a slave to pleasing others. You never experience the freedom of being yourself and enjoying the blessings God has uniquely given to you.

Israel demanded God to give them a king because they wanted to be like other nations. They chose to have a man rule over them rather than God. How much did this choice cost them? The kings oppressed the people, divided the kingdom, and led Israel astray from the statutes of God. As a result, the very pagan nations that Israel wanted to imitate enslaved them.

How could Israel choose an earthly king over the King of all kings to rule them? Well, how many times have we chosen to please our peers above pleasing

> *Any counsel that does not align with the Word of God is not worth hearing. Sometimes people blindly follow ungodly counsel simply because it provides a quick and easy solution or seems to lead to success.*

God? In our pursuit of acceptance and significance among our peers, we allow others, instead of God, to shape our lives and destinies. As believers, the LORD expects us to honor Him as Lord over every aspect of our lives.

Instant Gratification

Apparently, some people base their life decisions on their cravings. They constantly seek satisfaction at a snap of their fingers. *"If it feels good, do it,"* they say. What they do not tell you is that feel-good lifestyles carry long-term consequences.

Adam and Eve chose to indulge in fruit that pleased their eyes at the expense of a divine relationship with God. Even though they enjoyed the sweetness of the fruit at the time, afterwards they suffered the long-term consequences of separation from God, His provision, and His favor in the Garden of Eden.

> Jesus Said
> *"Be on your guard against all kinds of greed"*
> (Luke 12:15 NIV).

At times people compromise their faith because they want to enjoy the instant gratification of the flesh. Infidelity has destroyed marriages and families. Financial greed has robbed people of good jobs or even their freedom. Whenever people allow discontent with what they have to distort their perception, they become vulnerable to seeking instant gratification. They live for the short-term pleasure of their greed, only to face the long-term consequence of their poor choices. Jesus said, *"Be on your guard against all kinds of greed"* (Luke 12:15 NIV).

Misguided Counsel

Our source of counsel affects the choices we make. The people close to us or those we respect have more influence in our lives than we think. We rely on them for counsel when we get to the crossroads of life and are not sure which path to take. If our friends or our role models couldn't care less about having a close relationship with God, they won't seek God's counsel in their decision making. Those who idolize Hollywood celebrities will always be torn between living a lifestyle that is guided by the world and that which is of God. Psalm 1:1-2 (NIV) says it all: *"Blessed is the man who does not walk in the counsel of the wicked or stand in the way of sinners or sit in the seat of mockers. But his delight is in the law of the Lord."*

When Rehoboam, son of King Solomon, was crowned the king of Israel, he rejected the counsel of wise men and sought the counsel of his young friends. They advised him to rule over the people with tyranny and no sympathy. When Rehoboam followed their advice, the people rebelled against him, and he lost the entire kingdom that he had inherited.

Any counsel that does not align with the Word of God is not worth hearing. Sometimes people blindly follow ungodly counsel simply because it provides a quick and easy solution or seems to lead to success. For instance, some people use deception or bribery in order to get ahead in business, and then they cover the business in prayer. But becoming successful after gracing such unjust ways with prayers does not mean God approved the sin. As far as God is concerned, the end does not justify the means.

Unbridled Emotions

Emotions are part of all human beings. We experience both positive and negative emotions daily, and how we respond to them affects our judgment. Emotions can drive us to do some things that we would normally not do without provocation. For example, when we see a person in great need, our hearts fill with compassion. This emotion causes us to reach out and help. On the other hand, angry words can provoke unbridled anger, which can drive us to say or do things which harm other people. Think of the many wonderful relationships that harsh words or hurtful actions have broken. Proverbs 15:1 says, *"A harsh word stirs up anger."*

> *Going by mere emotions can lead us to make wrong decisions. We have to balance our feelings with careful thought in every decision. In fact, the key to making good judgments is to temper our emotions with facts.*

Some emotions trigger excitement in us. Some Christians dismiss such emotions as mere carnality, but we need to ask ourselves why God gave us such emotions. The reality is that the Bible shows us many people who expressed what they felt; among them was Jesus, who lived a sinless life.

Matthew 9:36: *"When he [Jesus] saw the crowds, he had compassion on them."*

John 11:35: *"Jesus wept."*

Perhaps what is more important is not how we feel but how we respond to those feelings. When it comes to making wise decisions in life, good feelings alone are not sufficient; in fact, they can easily lead us astray.

25

Unfortunately, many people today choose a spouse based on feelings alone. So when the feelings go, the marriage also goes. A healthy marriage relationship takes more than fuzzy feelings. It is a lifetime commitment to another person regardless of feelings alone.

Going by mere emotions can lead us to make wrong decisions. We have to balance our feelings with careful thought in every decision. In fact, the key to making good judgments is to temper our emotions with facts. Facts will weed out unwise decisions derived solely from feelings. For instance, one person may fall in love with another person. However, time and experience reveal that the other person is abusive, lacking self-control and character. Regardless of strong feelings of love on either part, these two people should not marry. Failure to face the facts will lead to an abusive marriage.

> *Going by mere emotions can lead us to make wrong decisions. We have to balance our feelings with careful thought in every decision.*

Even when we must deal with difficult situations, we need to keep our emotions in check. We should not allow negative emotions to control our responses. We can change our circumstances only by how we act, not how we feel. We must do what is right and stick by our actions in spite of our emotions. Acknowledging our emotions while we temper them with truth will help us plough ourselves out of hard situations.

We can find consolation in the fact that the fulfillment of God's promises in our lives does not depend on our emotions. We can fully rely on God's Word to take us through difficult times, even when our emotions are down. Psalm 145:13 (NIV) says: *"The Lord is faithful to all his promises and loving toward all he has made."*

Identity Crisis

If you do not know who you are, you will always try to be someone else. Identity crisis is a big issue, especially in the world today. Sadly, some people cannot figure out their gender; they do not know whether they are men or women. What a sad tragedy! Although most people do not struggle with gender identity, many do struggle with personality, physical appearance, background, or even social status. These struggles reveal the deep, underlying identity issues that people battle.

> *God intended us to find our identity in Him. So we ought to be who He created us to be, not what we wish we were or what others think we should be…God sees the original plans for your life; He sees your destiny.*

Sometimes people view their personality traits, whether they are introverts or extroverts, as detriments. Although each personality trait has strengths and weaknesses, God gave us these traits, as well as our physical features, ethnicities, and backgrounds, for a specific purpose. Psalm 139:14-16 describes how the LORD uniquely created each of us. *"I am fearfully and wonderfully made; marvelous are Your works … Your eyes saw my substance, being yet unformed. And in Your book they all were written, the days fashioned for me, when as yet there were none of them."*

27

God made us all to walk different paths in life. We are all as different and unique as the stars in the skies. Psalm 147:4 says: *"He counts the number of the stars; He calls them all by name."* And 1 Corinthians 15:41 says: *"For one star differs from another star in glory."* Because our endlessly creative God created each of us individually, we have different tastes and preferences, different personalities, and different passions in life.

So only you can do most effectively the work that God has called you to fulfill. God uniquely made you with the peculiar qualities, traits, and features that match His will for your life. God knew exactly what He was doing when He made you exactly the way you are.

> *When we have insufficient information about a matter, we cannot make a wise judgment about it.*

In the Bible, God used people with different personalities and from different walks of life to fulfill His purposes. Moses was a withdrawn, meek man who often felt inferior. Peter was a people person with a bit of a temper who wasn't afraid to speak his mind. Although these biblical characters sometimes faltered, they did great things for God. Moses led the Israelites out of Egypt, while Peter successfully headed the early church. Accepting and being proud of the person God created you to be will set you free from the heavy burden of trying to imitate someone else or make decisions based on other people's options. God wants to use you, not you pretending to be someone else.

God intended us to find our identity in Him. So we ought to be who He created us to be, not what we wish we were or what others think we should be. Other people can only see your past. But God sees the original plans for your life; He sees your destiny. When men saw Saul, they saw a murderer, but God saw a great minister of the gospel who would preach to the Gentiles. As a young man, the Israelites saw David as just a shepherd; but God saw him as a mighty warrior and a great king. Seek your identity in God, and your life will never be the same again.

Chapter 2

Take Responsibility

Taking responsibility for the wrong choices you make is very important. Failure to take responsibility for your wrong choices will affect not only you, but also your children. When Abraham went down to Egypt, he lied to Pharaoh that Sarah was his sister (Read Genesis 12:10-13). Years later, when Abraham's son Isaac went to Gerar, he too lied to the men in Gerar that Rebekah was his sister (Read Genesis 26:7). Some may call this repetition a generational curse, but it's not; Isaac simply did what he had learned from his father. Even though Isaac wasn't born at the time Abraham was in Egypt, he had at least heard about his father's shrewd escape from Pharaoh.

Unless you learn differently, you will usually act in the same way you saw your parents or guardians act while you were growing up. But God wants us to take responsibility for our mistakes and use His divine Word to lead us in the right path. The following four steps can help you take responsibility for the wrong choices you have made.

Admit Your Mistakes

Quit blaming others for your problems, and admit your own shortcomings. If you do not admit your mistakes, you will never receive the power from God to resolve the struggles you have.

Some people complain constantly. Even when someone offers a solution to their struggles, they still see a problem to the solution. Each time they get a new job, join a new church, or move to a new neighborhood, they complain that somebody doesn't like them or that the place just isn't right for them. I have come to learn that if John has a problem with everybody, maybe John is the problem. If we want to deal with our problems, then we must take responsibility for our mistakes.

Let's face it: although we are Spirit-filled believers, we still deal with sin. Sometimes we do what we shouldn't be doing, even though we know we shouldn't be doing it. We would love to call our wrongdoings weaknesses, but the Bible calls them sin. Unfortunately, many Christians do not know how to deal with sin; that helplessness is why they would rather ostracize someone from fellowship than deal with his sin. Because of their incompetence in dealing with sin, many Christians would rather live in hypocrisy than face alienation from their fellow believers.

> If we want to deal with our problems, then we must take responsibility for our mistakes.

The Bible states in 1 John 1:8: *If we say that we have no sin, we deceive ourselves, and the truth is not in us.* The apostle John, who was writing to believers, specifically addressed the need to deal with sin. He says that admitting we have sinned and repenting are the first steps to taking responsibility for our wrong choices in life.

> *No matter how ugly your sin, you can receive God's forgiveness if you seek it. Though people might not forgive you and might even alienate you, their reaction doesn't mean that God has not forgiven you. God's forgiveness is always independent of man's forgiveness.*

A rough childhood experience may plague your memory, or other people may have hurt you badly at some point in your life. As deeply as these very painful experiences may have affected your life, God does not want you to dwell in your past. According to Him, your past does not determine your future. You can choose to allow God to heal your wounded soul and dissolve your grudge against those who hurt you. Trying to justify your condition will not make you any better. Even though you may be a victim of circumstances, refusing to allow divine forgiveness into your heart will only keep you from experiencing the freedom that God wants you to have so that you may fulfill your God-given purpose in life.

Accept God's Forgiveness

32

What happens to that believer in the Lord who has sinned and now faces the consequences of that sin? How do you respond to the teenage Christian girl who had a child out of wedlock? How do you approach the preacher or the spiritual leader who is deep in sin? Sadly, some believers will stop fellowshipping with you even after you have admitted your sin and repented of it. But how does God deal with the believers who sin? Can they find forgiveness? Thank God, His Word has the final authority in our lives, not man. 1 John 1:9 states that *if we confess our sins, he is faithful and just and will forgive us our sins and purify us from all unrighteousness.*

> *Sometimes, the mistakes we make in life have great consequences. Turning around can be very humbling, but it is not the worst that could happen. Failing to reverse course will create more consequences and worsen the situation.*

People like to categorize sin into the small sins that everyone can just overlook and the big sins that bring shame to the church. The problem with this attitude is that it is more concerned about protecting an image than restoring a straying soul. From God's perspective, sin is sin. He has the same solution for all kinds of sins. Therefore, no matter how large or small you consider the sin you commit to be, the Lord says that if you confess it to Him, He will forgive you and make you clean and whole again.

No matter how ugly your sin, you can receive God's forgiveness if you seek it. Though people might not forgive you and might even alienate you, their reaction doesn't mean that God has not forgiven you. God's forgiveness is always independent of man's forgiveness.

As a born-again Christian, you do not have to live in the bondage of guilt any more. God is still in the business of forgiving and restoring the soul that strays away. God wants you to accept His forgiveness. Don't let the devil or men torment you with guilt for your past sins. God already forgave you. He has no record of your past sins. Corrie Ten Boom put it this way: _When God forgives you, He buries your sins in the sea of forgetfulness; He then puts a sign on the bank which says: NO FISHING ALLOWED._ Do not go back to find your past sins. The devil relishes using the weapon of condemnation to keep you from experiencing the freedom of forgiveness and new life in God.

Though you may face the consequences of your sins, NEVER interpret those consequences to mean that God has not forgiven you. If you committed a crime and you repented, God has forgiven you for your sin; however, you will still have to pay the full price of justice in a court of law. Don't blame God for the consequences of your mistakes. Instead, take full responsibility for the mistakes, and God will give you the grace to deal with the consequences. In fact, He will turn these stumbling blocks into stepping stones that will bless your life.

Amend Your Mistakes

When we get lost, the most logical thing we can do to get back on track is to turn around. Sometimes, the mistakes we make in life have great consequences. Turning around can be very humbling, but it is not the worst that could happen. Failing to reverse course will create more consequences and worsen the situation. Only turning around and going in the right direction will help you get your life back on the right path.

The LORD wants you to amend your mistakes when you accept His forgiveness. Asking God for forgiveness will do you no good if you go right back to making the same wrong choices. But how can you amend your mistakes?

The devil doesn't like for people to be accountable to one another; he knows that the power of accountability thwarts his wicked plans. He always seeks to prey on those believers who isolate themselves.

The first step is to realize that God has given you the ability to overcome the sin you are battling. According to 1 Corinthians 10:13, God will not allow you to face a greater temptation than you can handle. He also assures you that He will provide a way to overcome temptations. If you do not ask Him for help, you will always feel helpless about your situation.

The next step to amending your mistakes is staying away from those environments or influences that tempt you to make wrong choices. Do not make yourself vulnerable. If your past mistakes resulted from unhealthy relationships, stay away from those relationships. No matter how spiritual you might be, you are not invincible. Set limits and boundaries to protect you from being lured by the evil schemes of the devil. Why did God command the Israelites not to mingle with the Canaanites? He knew that mingling with ungodly people would tempt His children to act in ungodly ways.

Amending past mistakes does not mean undoing what you have already done; erasing every consequence is impossible to do. Instead, do whatever you must not to repeat the same mistakes again. So it is never too late to amend your mistakes. If anything, through correcting past mistakes you gain the wisdom to deal with future challenges.

The final step to amending your mistakes is beginning to do the right things. Whenever the apostle Paul instructed believers to get rid of certain vices, he also admonished them to pursue good virtues. _Put off, concerning your former conduct, the old man which grows corrupt according to the deceitful lusts, and be renewed in the spirit of your mind, and that you put on the new man which was created according to God, in true righteousness and holiness_ (Ephesians 4:22-24). Failing to replace sin with virtue leaves a vacuum that tempts you to fall back into the old pattern of sin; you must both let go of ungodly desires and hold on to godly virtues.

When you engage in God's Word, you will know the right things to do to lead a victorious Christian life. And when you know what is right, do it, no matter what it costs. You'll surely be glad to have made the right choice. Do not let your past mistakes and failures keep you from pursuing God's best for you.

Be Accountable to Somebody

When you have taken the first three steps of taking responsibility for your mistakes, ask someone who is spiritually mature to keep you accountable. Choose someone who will encourage you and pray with you in moments when you feel vulnerable. Confessing and praying with someone you trust will help you stay strong in the midst of trials and temptations. The Bible says that being together is better than being alone, because two friends can help each other (Read Ecclesiastes 4:9-10).

The devil doesn't like for people to be accountable to one another; he knows that the power of accountability thwarts his wicked plans. He always seeks to prey on those believers who isolate themselves. In fact, most financial or sexual scandals result from a lack of accountability. When you invite a wise mentor into your life, he or she will warn you ahead of time when the enemy sets a snare on your path. The godly kings of Judah followed this principle when they consulted the prophets of God, who held them accountable to God's Word.

> *Unless you learn differently, you will usually act in the same way you saw your parents or guardians act while you were growing up.*

Do not fear to take responsibility for the wrong choices you have made in your life. Shouldering that responsibility will help you heal from your past and turn your previous wrong choices into opportunities for growth and maturity.

Chapter 3

Confront Your Past

Although you cannot forget your painful past experiences or mistakes, you can certainly find healing and restoration in Christ. Your past does not have to hold you captive or haunt you; God wants to set you free. With God, your future is secure despite your unpleasant experiences. As far as He is concerned, your future is more important than your past. He does not judge you based on your past; neither does He change His wonderful plans for your life because of your past mistakes. Whether you are dealing with the consequences of past sins or the pain of rejection, fear, or low self-esteem,

> *With God, your future is secure despite your unpleasant experiences.*

God wants you to conquer these troubles by boldly confronting them. He desires you to live a meaningful, joyful, and victorious life.

Confront False Guilt

False guilt is blaming ourselves for sins or mistakes we have already been forgiven. Many people have a difficult time forgiving themselves. In fact, they feel they do not deserve happy lives and accept every bad experience or disappointment as fate. God wants those who come to Him to begin new, victorious lives, even if they were previously irresponsible, promiscuous, or addicted to alcohol or drugs. The Bible says, *The thief does not come except to steal, and to kill, and to destroy. I have come that they may have life, and that they may have it more abundantly* (John 10:10). God wants you to lead a successful life and enjoy the abundant life He promised without feeling guilty.

> *Therefore, there is now no condemnation for those who are in Christ Jesus.*
>
> (Romans 8:1)

False guilt does not come from God, but from Satan, *the accuser of brethren* (Read Revelation 12:10). Satan uses false guilt to keep us from overcoming our areas of vulnerability. But the Bible says, *Therefore, there is now no condemnation for those who are in Christ Jesus* (Romans 8:1). Through Christ, your sins are forgiven. The apostle John declares that the believers overcame the accuser, the devil, *by the blood of the Lamb and by the word of their testimony* (Revelation 12:9-11).

Christ's blood covers all sins; so keep testifying that you are forgiven. Once you understand that God no longer holds you guilty of what He has already forgiven, you can confidently move forward without letting your previous failures hold you back.

Confront Rejection

Feelings of rejection may stem from the death of a loved one, physical or verbal abuse (especially from parents or guardians), or physical or emotional abandonment (again, especially by a parent or guardian). Although the pain of losing a loved one through death is emotionally traumatizing, it is much easier to accept than the other forms of rejection. In fact, studies show that children of divorced parents struggle more in life than those of deceased parents.

People who struggle with rejection have a difficult time building healthy relationships. They are often paranoid about being rejected by others. This obstacle is one of great concern, because God created humans as social beings. If anything, living in isolation is difficult. Every day we mingle with people at work, school, church, or the wider community; avoiding people completely is impossible. Having been hurt by people close to us doesn't mean that no one else can earn our trust.

> _Therefore, isolation should not be an option for dealing with rejection. This lonely path will lead you into a downward spiral of depression._

If you fear rejection, first and foremost God wants you to recognize that He has not rejected you. He has your best interests at heart. Solomon says that _there is a friend who sticks closer than a brother_ (Proverbs 18:24), one whom you can trust when all others fail you. This friend is God, who promises that *He will never leave you nor forsake you* (Deuteronomy 31:8 NIV). He also assures you that *I took you from the ends of the earth, from its farthest corners I called you. I said, 'You are my servant'; I have chosen you and have not rejected you. So do not fear, for I am with you; do not be dismayed, for I am your God. I will strengthen you and help you; I will uphold you with my righteous right hand* (Isaiah 41:9-10 NIV).

You need to take God at His word when He says that He truly loves you. As you develop your relationship with God, you will build your trust in Him. You will come to realize in time that you are never alone.

> *Living in fear is not the will of God for you. You need to understand that fear does not come from God. He wants you to know that you can do all things through Christ who strengthens [you] (Philippians 4:13).*

Therefore, isolation should not be an option for dealing with rejection. This lonely path will lead you into a downward spiral of depression. The Bible says that *two are better than one, because they have a good reward for their labor* (Ecclesiastes 4:9). Ask God to lead you to an emotionally healthy person who can walk with you through the recovery process. Choose to trust this person, even in situations which trigger paranoid feelings. Building a relationship with someone who is emotionally healthy provides you not only with good support but also with an example to emulate.

Confront Fear

Courage is not the absence of fear, but the presence of faith to confront fear. We all face fear at some point, but how we deal with it is what matters most. Franklin D. Roosevelt was right when he said, _The only thing we have to fear is fear itself._

Fear paralyzes us and keeps us from achieving our life goals. The more we give in to it, the more it controls us. Inside each of us is great potential, but the fear of failure keeps us from exploring our hidden abilities. Failure is not the worst thing that can happen to us; the failure to attempt great things due to fear is far worse. Successful people in life are not successful because they have never failed or feared. They are successful because they never stopped trying. In life, there is no victory without a battle. Sometimes, you have to fight more than once to win.

As we discuss confronting fear, we will identify some of the symptoms of fear. For instance, if you nearly always respond negatively to solutions or new ideas, you probably have a failure mentality that says, "I will fail no matter what I do" or, "It cannot be done." People who are controlled by fear expect failure even before they try, and sure enough, they often fulfill their expectations. The Bible says, _For God has not given us a spirit of fear, but of power and of love and of a sound mind_ (2 Timothy 1:7).

Living in fear is not the will of God for you. You need to understand that fear does not come from God. He wants you to know that you _can do all things through Christ who strengthens [you]_ (Philippians 4:13).

Another symptom of fear is avoiding challenges, even when they lead to greater opportunities. In order to

42

overcome this fear, we need to change our focus from the challenge to the wonderful opportunities ahead. A tightrope acrobat who was once asked about the secret to his exceptional balance responded, *keeping my eyes on where I want to go.*

When we set our eyes on the opportunities awaiting us, the courage to face our challenges will arise within us. Therefore, learn to focus on Christ; He will give you the courage to face any mountain. *Let us fix our eyes on Jesus, the author and perfecter of our faith, who for the joy set before him endured the cross, scorning its shame, and sat down at the right hand of the throne of God* (Hebrews 12:2 NIV).

> *Sometimes, God will not instantly take away our problems; instead, He may choose to take us through a process of change that comes in stages and takes time.*

What motivates you to work hard? Are you only trying to keep yourself from failure or maintain what you have; or are you striving for success? The former attitude reveals fear, while the latter reveals courage. Achievers are more concerned about winning than losing. They work harder because passion for success drives them. Most of our fears are unfounded. Did you know that eighty percent of what we fear never happens? God wants you to attempt the great things He has planned for you with victory in mind: *But thanks be to God, who gives us the victory through our Lord Jesus Christ* (1 Corinthians 15:57).

Just as painful experiences develop fear, triumph develops courage. Facing our fears by doing exactly what we fear is the key to breaking the power of fear. Most of our fears exist more in the mind than in reality. The Lord said to Joshua, _Have I not commanded you? Be strong and of good courage; do not be afraid, nor be dismayed, for the LORD your God is with you wherever you go_ (Joshua 1:9). When we identify the past victories God has given us, we will develop the courage to face other challenges. David knew this very well when he offered to face Goliath. He said to King Saul, _Your servant has killed both lion and bear; and this uncircumcised Philistine will be like one of them, seeing he has defied the armies of the living God_ (1 Samuel 17:36).

Confront Low Self-Esteem

Low self-esteem can derive from put-downs and unwarranted criticism. Unfortunately, demeaning criticism is rampant in our society, contributing to widespread low self-esteem. People struggling with low self-esteem tend to blame themselves, even when the criticism is not their fault. Parents sometimes do not realize the serious consequences for their children when they speak negative things about them, and worse still, when they openly criticize them before others. This terrible verbal damage instills life-long low self-confidence in a child.

People struggling with low self-esteem tend to compare themselves with others. They often base their self-worth on how they measure up to others. If someone seems better than they consider themselves to be, they feel worthless. They only feel good if they perceive themselves to be better than someone else.

If you engage in this kind of comparison, you must understand that this notion is distorted and wrong, because who you are has nothing to do with who others are. Accepting who you are is the key to building your self-esteem and confidence. Being different from others is okay; in fact, your differences make you unique and valuable in society.

Those who have low self-esteem tend to personalize their mistakes. They believe that the mistakes they have made define them. They cannot separate who they are from what they have done. But failing once or even a few times doesn't make someone a failure. A person who is able to separate who he is and what he has done will be able to resolve his mistakes without judging himself unjustly. God does not expect people to keep wallowing in depression because of their mistakes. People who attempt great things are susceptible to making mistakes. If you have made mistakes, God wants you to learn from them and move on.

> *If the Israelites could not trust God in the desert, how could they trust Him in the Promised Land where they had to face giants? God wants to develop us spiritually so that we will be able to keep the blessings He gives us.*

Another aspect of building your self-esteem is identifying your areas of strength. No one is good at everything. However, just like everyone else, you have areas of strength where you thrive. You have something to offer to others which they don't have. When you recognize your inner strengths, you will gain confidence in realizing that you can make a difference in your life and the lives of others.

Overcoming low self-esteem requires us to recognize that what others think or say about us, our background, our current situation, or our social status does not determine our self-worth. So often we allow hurtful words and attitudes to determine who we are. But only God determines our self-worth. He assures us that we are valuable to Him. _For thus says the LORD of hosts: 'He sent Me after glory, to the nations which plunder you; for he who touches you touches the apple of His eye'_ (Zechariah 2:8). If we are so precious and valuable to God, why should we undermine ourselves? When we see ourselves as God see us, we gain a whole new perspective of who we are and what we can accomplish.

> _The key to setting limits with others is being honest with them. Let them know what makes you uncomfortable, what you do not like, or what deeply offends you._

Have Realistic Expectations

If you have not made up your mind to deal with your past, going from one deliverance or prayer service to another will do you no good. You have to be up to the task of making tough changes after praying about your issues. Prayer is an important part of the process of change, but it is only the beginning. Many people stop with prayer and wonder why things haven't changed.

When the children of Israel were trapped between the Red Sea and the Egyptian soldiers, they cried to God to take action, but instead the LORD challenged them to take action. _And the LORD said to Moses, 'Why do you cry to Me? Tell the children of Israel to go forward. But lift up your rod, and stretch out your hand over the sea and divide it. And the children of Israel shall go on dry ground through the midst of the sea,'_ (Exodus 14:15-16). If you want to experience deliverance, put your faith into action by taking the necessary steps to effect change.

Sometimes, God will not instantly take away our problems; instead, He may choose to take us through a process of change that comes in stages and takes time. If the children of Israel had used the shortest route to get to Canaan, the journey would have taken them less than forty days. But the LORD chose to take them through a long and unfamiliar route. Through God's path, those who chose to obey God willingly learned to trust God for provision, protection, and guidance. Learning this lesson was essential for possessing the land of Canaan. If the Israelites could not trust God in the desert, how could they trust Him in the Promised Land where they had to face giants? God wants to develop us spiritually so that we will be able to keep the blessings He gives us.

When you are dealing with your past, you need to remember that change takes time. Be patient with yourself, and do not give up when you falter. *My brethren, count it all joy when you fall into various trials, knowing that the testing of your faith produces patience. But let patience have its perfect work, that you may be perfect and complete, lacking nothing* (James 1:2-4).

Set Boundaries

When you visit a zoo, you probably notice that specific boundaries enclose the animals. Though some may look harmless and docile, they have wild instincts, and they could easily attack when provoked. The cage or fence exists to protect you from harm. On the other hand, some animals are timid and quite vulnerable. For them, the enclosure exists to protect them from predators.

Setting boundaries in our lives will protect us not only from the snares of past addictions and fears but also from trespassers. We all need to set several boundaries in our lives.

Past Addictions

Every vehicle has gauges on the dashboard to alert the driver on the condition of the car. They monitor the speed, fuel level, and engine temperature. The vehicle also has lights marked "oil" and "check engine" that turn red when the oil is low or the engine is faulty. The driver bears the responsibility of checking the gauges. Failing to check them or ignoring them could mean a stalled vehicle or, worse still, an accident. Those gauges serve as warnings.

Once you understand that God no longer holds you guilty of what He has already forgiven, you can confidently move forward without letting your previous failures hold you back.

In the same way, we need gauges in our lives to warn us when we get near the danger zone of our past addictions. These gauges should help us to stay away from places, things, or people who may lure us back to our past addictions. We must avoid situations that trigger temptations. For a former alcoholic, staying away from people ensnared by this addiction will keep you at a safe distance.

Areas of Vulnerability

Some things that we do are not necessarily bad. If anything, they are very important for our overall well-being. However, if we use them in excess, they become hazardous. For instance, we all need to eat every day, but if we consume excessive food, we are likely to be obese and develop health problems. Another example is TV and video games, which are wonderful tools for entertainment. However, studies show that kids who spend hours each day on these gadgets have a short attention span, which affects their ability to learn in a classroom setting.

> *People struggling with low self-esteem tend to compare themselves with others. They often base their self-worth on how they measure up to others.*

For substances or activities which are not inherently harmful, we base our boundaries on times and quantities. If we learn to set limits for those things we enjoy, we will become healthier people who are better at self-control. But if we neglect these limits, the very things we enjoy will control us.

Relationships

We also need to set boundaries around our interaction with some people. Putting the interests of others first is wonderful; however we should guard ourselves against surrendering our peace, our destinies, and the deepest desires of our hearts to manipulative and controlling people. When we don't set rational, healthy boundaries, we become vulnerable to people who like taking advantage of others, and we enable them to abuse us. We all have a personal responsibility to protect ourselves and those under our care.

The key to setting limits with others is being honest with them. Let them know what makes you uncomfortable, what you do not like, or what deeply offends you. By doing so, you let them know the areas in your life where they cannot trespass. The Bible says in Deuteronomy 32:8: *When the Most High divided their inheritance to the nations, when He separated the sons of Adam, He set the boundaries of the peoples according to the number of the children of Israel.* In order to avoid conflict among the people, the LORD ensured that the sons of Adam knew the boundaries of their land.

The Bible sets boundaries for us in areas of relationships, business, personal life, and many other issues for specific reasons, and we should never ignore these limits. Sometimes people assume that God set these boundaries to keep them from enjoying life. After all, some people get a thrill from pushing the limits to see how far they can go without crashing disastrously into a catastrophe. But what they do not realize is that God put boundaries in place to protect us; His laws are His boundaries. When we break them, we face awful consequences.

In Deuteronomy 28:1-2, 15 the Bible lists not only the blessings of obeying God's laws but also the consequences of disobeying them. *If you fully obey the LORD your God and carefully follow all his commands I give you today, the LORD your God will set you high above all the nations on earth. All these blessings will come upon you and accompany you if you obey the LORD your God . . . However, if you do not obey the LORD your God and do not carefully follow all his commands and decrees I am giving you today, all these curses will come upon you and overtake you . . .* (NIV).

Imagine the many fatal accidents that would never have occurred if only the drivers had obeyed traffic laws. The government establishes traffic laws to prevent tragic accidents. In the same way, the boundaries you set in your life will protect you from vulnerable situations and seal any loopholes the enemy may use to attack you.

The Serenity Prayer

*God grant me the serenity
to accept the things I cannot change;
courage to change the things I can;
and wisdom to know the difference...*

Reinhold Niebuhr

Chapter 4

Change the Way You Think

The mind is the most powerful part of a human being. The mind conceives, processes, and communicates thoughts to the rest of the body, which acts on them. Our minds influence our thoughts, emotions, actions, and behavior. What is on our minds reveals who we are, why we are where we are, and why we do what we do, and it predicts where we will be in the future. In essence, the contents of our minds reveal our general perspective of life.

The way you think affects not only you but also the world around you. It will either contribute to your well-being and that of others or cause negative consequences in your life. People who have a pessimistic mindset focus more on bad news than good news. When pessimists act on their negative perspective, their mentality produces negative results. On the contrary, optimistic people rise above their circumstances to become successful. Their positive attitude can see beyond their immediate situations; so they can act positively.

Stop Believing Lies

But what really influences the way we think? Whether we realize it or not, what people say about us markedly influences how we perceive ourselves. Many people struggle with negative judgments from a peer, a parent, or some other authority. Words are powerful; they can either build or destroy. The Bible says, *The tongue has the power of life and death* (Proverbs 18:21). This power explains why people still talk about the negative remarks they heard while growing up, such remarks as, "You will never amount to anything," or, "You can't do anything right," or, "You are such a failure," or, "Why can't you be like your brother/sister?"

> *The way you think affects not only you but also the world around you. It will either contribute to your well-being and that of others or cause negative consequences in your life.*

These words still haunt the adults who heard them as children. But what is worse is that they believe they are not valuable and accept failure as their destiny. Years afterwards, people still believe outright lies about them. These lies cause them to live at the end of an imaginary leash that keeps them from going where they have the strength and intelligence to go. In other words, someone else set false boundaries for them, and they have stayed inside the narrow space of those lies.

Do not let other people limit what you can do. God never created victims; do not allow negative people to make you one. God sees you as His child (Read John 1:12). He says that He has a wonderful plan for your life (Read Jeremiah 29:11). He sees you as a victor, not a victim (Read Romans 8:37). He sees you as a vessel He can use (Read 2 Timothy 2:20-21). All the negative things you have heard about yourself are the enemy's lies, which he designed to keep you from becoming all that God intended you to be.

> *Problems are inevitable, but your attitude determines how you respond to them. While some people see problems in every situation, others see opportunities in challenges.*

If you want to destroy the lies you believe about yourself, you must change the way you think. Use God's Word to find what God truly says about you in order to identify the lies you've believed all these years. Jesus said, *You will know the truth, and the truth will set you free* (John 8:32). Do not live a lie, because Christ already paid the price for your victory. God wants you to succeed, just as He created you to do.

What He says about you is superior to what anyone else says. In fact, no mistake or tragedy can change God's plan for your life. Believe what God says about you, and the truth will change your life.

Fight the Battle of the Mind

Life is full of different trials and challenges. And on top of the obstacles we encounter, self-defeating negative thoughts and positive thoughts constantly fight a vicious battle in our minds. We can choose to yield to either the negative thoughts or the positive thoughts. Although negative thoughts always strive to dominate the positive thoughts in our minds, we are totally responsible for the thoughts we think, and we must choose to confront negative thoughts daily if we want to win the battle of the mind. According to Scripture, God always thinks wonderful thoughts about us. We should think the same way about ourselves if we want to lead triumphant lives.

The Bible says, *For as he [a man] thinks in his heart [mind], so is he* (Proverbs 23:7). Since the doorway to a man's heart is through his mind, we must guard the thoughts we process, because if we meditate on negative thoughts, we will act on them. On the other hand, if we choose to meditate on positive, hope-building thoughts, they will shape our lives and futures in a great way.

Change Your Attitude

Problems are inevitable, but your attitude determines how you respond to them. While some people see problems in every situation, others see opportunities in challenges. Two people can face the same challenge but react in totally different ways based on how they perceive the challenge. One may see his challenge as a stepping stone to a new level, while the other may view it as an immovable roadblock.

Joseph's brothers sold him as a slave. Joseph could have decided that God had forsaken him and lost all hope of ever realizing his dream. His circumstances could have buried him in depression. But Joseph chose to see his challenge as an opportunity to put his skills and gifts to work. He focused on what God had revealed to him. His positive attitude led him from the pit to the palace.

On the other hand, God dramatically freed the Israelites from their oppressors in Egypt. They could have taken heart in the power of God. They could have focused only on their destination in the Promised Land. But a journey from Egypt to Canaan that should have lasted only several days took the Israelites forty years, all because they set their minds on their prevailing wilderness circumstances rather than on God.

> *For the word of God is living and active. Sharper than any double-edged sword, it penetrates even to dividing soul and spirit, joints and marrow; it judges the thoughts and attitudes of the heart (Hebrews 4:12 NIV).*

Success or failure always depends much more on the mind than outward circumstances. People who have a positive attitude of faith will envision victory even in the midst of negative circumstances. Those with positive attitudes turn their trials into testimonies and their sufferings into success. From God's perspective, every circumstance is an opportunity to grow in faith. Choosing to focus on God's grace, love, and mercy transforms every situation into an opportunity for pursuing a God-given purpose in life.

Think Empowering Thoughts

Have you ever considered that every great achievement or success began with a thought? We live in the era of information and technology. Just think about the invention of the Internet, which has revolutionized the world of communication. You can do business or access information anywhere in the world at the click of a mouse right in the comfort of your home. This excellent, multi-billion-dollar industry began with an innovative idea.

Imagine how your life would look if you started empowering your mind with God's eternal Word. Scripture says: *For the word of God is living and active. Sharper than any double-edged sword, it penetrates even to dividing soul and spirit, joints and marrow; it judges the thoughts and attitudes of the heart* (Hebrews 4:12 NIV). God's Word has the ability to transform your life entirely. Allowing the Word of God to influence your mind will empower you to think and to do extraordinary things.

> *You cannot stop a bird from flying over your head, but you can surely stop it from building a nest in your hair.*
>
> Martin Luther

For us to empower our minds with God's Word, we must change our thinking patterns. The LORD wants us to stop thinking like victims and start thinking like victors. So we must renew our minds with Scripture. The apostle Paul gives us this challenge: *Do not be conformed to this world, but be transformed by the renewing of your mind, that you may prove what is that good and acceptable and perfect will of God* (Romans 12:2).

Renewing our minds means that we stop thinking self-defeating thoughts and start thinking positive, empowering, Christ-like thoughts instead. Our natural thinking limits us to our human abilities. However, God's Word breaks through our self-imposed barriers. David faced Goliath with the confidence that God would deliver Goliath into his hands (Read 1 Samuel 17:45-46). Conventional wisdom would have barred David from enlisting in the army, let alone facing a giant. But David wasn't relying on his natural abilities. He was relying on God and His Word. Like David, take the initiative to conquer negative beliefs and renew your mind with God's Word. If you do so, your life will never be the same.

> _These lies cause them to live at the end of an imaginary leash that keeps them from going where they have the strength and intelligence to go. In other words, someone else set false boundaries for them, and they have stayed inside the narrow space of those lies._

The process of renewing your mind requires you to filter your thoughts. On the settings of your browser, you can easily block X-rated material and advertisement from your email inbox. Email filters automatically send such material directly to the spam or junk mail folder to be deleted. In the same way, filtering all the thoughts that come to your mind will help you block and reject the evil, negative ones. As Martin Luther said, _You cannot stop a bird from flying over your head, but you can surely stop it from building a nest in your hair._ You cannot stop the devil from testing you with negative thoughts, but you can certainly stop his evil, negative thoughts from breeding in your mind.

The Bible says, _Finally, brothers, whatever is true, whatever is noble, whatever is right, whatever is pure, whatever is lovely, whatever is admirable—if anything is excellent or praiseworthy—think about such things_ (Philippians 4:8). Once you fill your mind with the powerful, righteous, positive thoughts found in God's Word, you will need to act on them. Unless you take action, getting new, empowering information will not change your life. Take the initiative to study the Word, meditate on it, and apply it in your life. What you think is what you speak, and what you speak is what you do. Therefore, apply God's Word in your mind, and it will change the way you think and live.

Chapter 5

Guard Against Making Wrong Choices

Taking responsibility for the wrong choices you've made and amending those mistakes is a great step, but we also need to keep from making those mistakes again. Failure to set boundaries that guard us will only result in the same vicious cycle of making wrong choices again. The following six steps will guard us against making wrong choices.

Seek First the Counsel of God

Some people struggle with allowing God to have total preeminence in their lives. They presume that involving God in their decisions means that God will ask them to do something they dislike or give up what they treasure most. They think that giving up their choices in favor of God's choices means living a miserable life. Because of this misconception, many people make major life decisions without first seeking the counsel of God. Only after they have made those decisions do they ask God to bless their plans. They only consult God when they get stranded or when their plans fail. It is no wonder we fight battles God did not intend for us to fight or lose battles God intended for us to win. God wants us to rely on His infinite wisdom so that we can make wise choices.

Sometimes people are quick to seize any opportunity that comes their way. After all, they reason, because some opportunities only come once in a lifetime, God must approve them. However, not every door of opportunity that opens before you is from God. Whether you're considering a high-paying job offer or a ministry door that could usher you into the limelight, you must seek the counsel of God first before pursuing any venture. The Bible says, *Seek first His [God's] kingdom and His righteousness, and all these things will be given to you as well (Matthew 6:33).* When we make God our first priority, He will help us to make wise choices that lead to a fulfilling life. God knows the unforeseen challenges, hurdles, and disappointments that we may not see.

> *Whether you are dealing with sour relationships, business issues, work-related stress, financial constraints, government issues, or health concerns, the Word of God offers counsel on how to deal with everything that affects your daily life.*

I have heard countless testimonies of Christian businesspeople who felt an inclination to turn down good business opportunities. Having made such a decision that seemed odd, they were later grateful to God when they learned that the business offer ended in bankruptcy. Seeking God's counsel in every decision is always for your own good.

Search God's Word

The Word of God contains His infinite wisdom on how to make wise choices. So whenever you don't know what choice to make in a confusing situation, you should search God's Word to learn what it says. No matter what predicament you face, God's Word will always be a lamp unto your feet and a light to your path to guide you in the right direction (Read Psalm 119:105). Whether you are dealing with sour relationships, business issues, work-related stress, financial constraints, government issues, or health concerns, the Word of God offers counsel on how to deal with everything that affects your daily life. When you seek first the counsel of God by searching the Scriptures, you will find wisdom to guide you toward the right choice. Joshua said to the Israelites, *Do not let this book of the Law depart from your mouth; meditate on it day and night so that you may be careful to do everything written in it. Then you will be prosperous and successful* (Joshua 1:8 NIV).

> *Wise leaders always choose godly men to advise them and to pray with them. Find the godly people around you who made right choices when they faced the challenges you are now facing. Learn from them.*

The Word of God has a fivefold purpose. First, it instructs us on how to make wise choices. Second, it rebukes us whenever we make wrong choices. Third, it corrects us when we are wrong by guiding us back to the right path. Fourth, it shields us against making wrong choices. Fifth, it trains us to rely on the counsel of God in every aspect of our daily lives (Read 2 Timothy 3:16). From now on, read your Bible expecting to gain the wisdom you need to make the right choices in life that please God.

Ask God for Wisdom

James 1:5-6 counsels: *If any of you lack wisdom, he should ask God, who gives generously to all without finding fault, and it will be given to him* (NIV). The way to ask God for wisdom is through prayer, not grumbling. Unfortunately, sometimes we are quicker to grumble about our problems than we are to pray to God about our requests.

When the Israelites faced challenges in the wilderness, instead of praying to God to help them, they whined and complained to God about their circumstances. Instead of seeing God as their solution, they saw Him as the problem. As a result, they unwisely chose to follow idols. Even today, people blame God for the challenges they face. We often hear people say, "If God loved me, why did He let this happen to me?" Why do we insist on seeing God, not the devil, as the troublemaker?

God has a solution to every challenge that you face. However, you must communicate your requests to God through prayer in order to get solutions. As you pray, remember that you may not always get the answer that you expect, but you will surely get the solution that you need. God knows what is best for us. So let us receive His solution with thanksgiving, and He will satisfy us with good things (Psalm 145:16).

The apostle James admonished the believers that *you do not have, because you do not ask God. When you ask, you do not receive, because you ask with wrong motives, that you may spend what you get on your pleasure* (James 4:2-3 NIV). Before you request anything from God, search the motives of your heart. What you may be asking from God may be a right choice that aligns with God's Word. However, your motive for asking may not be right. When you pray for success in your ministry, business, or personal life, what is your motive? Do you want to prove yourself to others, gain popularity, or bring glory to God?

Be Sensitive to the Holy Spirit's Intuition

Sometimes choosing between the options life offers you is quite a challenge, especially when you have to choose between two good options. For instance, you may decide to trust God for a good job, a godly spouse, or a ministry opportunity, and somewhere down the road, multiple options come your way. They all look great and align with God's Word. How do you make the right choice?

> *Wise leaders always choose godly men to advise them and to pray with them. Find the godly people around you who made right choices when they faced the challenges you are now facing. Learn from them.*

When you reach such crossroads, always remember that your loving Father knows what is best for you. Therefore, through His Word, fervent prayer, and the intuition of His Spirit, He will guide you in making the right choice. If you have built a deep relationship with the LORD, you will be able to discern the leading of His Spirit.

When a certain pursuit is His will for you, the LORD will give you inner peace in your heart about it. On the other hand, your heart will feel unsettled about whatever is not the will of God. As you keep praying and searching His Word, He will guide you toward the right choices. Philippians 4:6-7(NIV) *Do not be anxious about anything, but in every situation, by prayer and petition, with thanksgiving, present your requests to God. ⁷ And the peace of God, which transcends all understanding, will guard your hearts and your minds in Christ Jesus.*

We should learn to distinguish burdens that are self-imposed, those that others impose on us, and those the LORD prompts us to bear. The burdens others impose on us, as well as those we assume alone, are heavy, troublesome, and oppressive.

Seek Godly Advice

Don't wait until you've made wrong choices to seek godly counsel. Wise leaders always choose godly men to advise them and to pray with them. Find the godly people around you who made right choices when they faced the challenges you are now facing. Learn from them.

The kings of Judah who had godly advisors reigned over the kingdom successfully. The Bible gives the account of King Uzziah. *He [Uzziah] did what was right in the eyes of the Lord just as his father Amaziah had done. He sought God during the days of Zechariah, who instructed him in the fear of God. As long as he sought the LORD, God gave him success* (2 Chronicles 26:4-5 NIV). The reason Uzziah succeeded was that he received godly counsel from Zechariah, who held him accountable to the Word of God. As long as Uzziah sought the counsel of God, he made right choices that led him to success.

Unfortunately, the reign of Uzziah did not end the way it began. When he stopped seeking the counsel of God, he became proud and arrogant. As a result, he made wrong choices that led to his downfall. Many people begin well in a new job, ministry, or relationship, but over time they stop seeking God consistently. Bob Reccord, in his book *Forged by Fire,* states that *the road to success can be a slippery slope to disaster; success is unfortunately bordered by the steep terrain of temptation and the seemingly bottomless canyons of immoral and unethical decisions.*

Accept this caution that seeking first the counsel of God should not be a seasonal issue. We should consistently make God our first priority every day of our lives.

Never make spontaneous decisions. Take time to think through the long-term effects. Ask yourself, "How will these choices affect me in the future?" When you first take time to seek the counsel of God through His Word, prayer, the guidance of His Spirit, and godly advice, you will guard yourself against making wrong choices.

Know Your Responsibility

Out of the goodness of their hearts, some people feel obligated to meet every need that they see. Although bearing the burdens of others is biblical, so is meeting the needs in your own house. God does not expect you personally to meet every need in the world. You are not God. He alone can carry the burdens of the world. You and I can only carry a certain amount of that burden. When we exceed our limits, the inevitable happens: we break down. The good works we do without God's direction end up hurting us. In the parable of the talent (Matthew 25:14-15), the Bible says that the master gave the servants talents according to their abilities. We can rest in the knowledge that God gives to both you and me various measures of responsibilities according to what we can handle.

People sometimes shoulder responsibilities because they do not want to feel guilty or hurt the feelings of others. In such cases, they do so at their expense or that of their family. They do not find any joy in what they do, and they suffer a great deal as well. We should learn to distinguish burdens that are self-imposed, those that others impose on us, and those the LORD prompts us to bear. The burdens others impose on us, as well as those we assume alone, are heavy, troublesome, and oppressive. To avoid bearing those burdens that are not our responsibility, we must learn to say: "I am sorry; I cannot help you," without feeling guilty. If we set correct priorities, we will not be overburdened.

Unfortunately, some people who have perfected the art of living off others do take advantage of them. They intentionally refuse to take care of their own responsibilities. They are good at getting others to bear those burdens. Though they are in no way victims of circumstance, they portray themselves as victims. The Bible gives this warning, *Do not take advantage of each other, but fear your God* (Leviticus 25:17). If we keep bailing out such people, we are only contributing to their bad behavior. Their main problem is not their needs but their failure to take responsibility, and the best help we can offer is to counsel them courteously on how they can resolve their issues. However, refusing such people does not excuse us from helping the poor or those with genuine needs. Galatians 2:10 (NIV) says that *we should continue to remember the poor.*

> *It is no wonder we fight battles God did not intend for us to fight or lose battles God intended for us to win. God wants us to rely on His infinite wisdom so that we can make wise choices.*

We have to be careful not to get involved in other people's business unless they invite us. Unsolicited advice can land us in problems. In the workplace, sometimes people meddle in the affairs of other departments. Although their intentions may be good, their involvement becomes a bone of contention to those in that department. The reality is that the issues of other departments are not their responsibility; therefore, they should stay out of them. The apostle Paul gives this admonition: *Make it your ambition to lead a quiet life, to mind your own business* (1 Thessalonians 4:11 NIV).

Knowing your responsibility will shield you from the distractions of other good or bad responsibilities. God wants you to stay focused on the responsibilities He has given you. In Matthew 11:29-30, Jesus said *Take My yoke upon you and learn from Me, for I am gentle and lowly in heart, and you will find rest for your souls. For My yoke is easy and My burden is light.*

Your goal in life should be to fulfill the responsibilities the Lord has entrusted to you. Such responsibilities are not burdensome but delightful and satisfying. Know your responsibilities, and stick to them.

Chapter 6

Guard Against Deception

Have you ever heard the saying, *"When the deal is too good, think twice"*? This simple yet profound adage offers great wisdom in guarding against deception. Deception is one of the schemes the devil uses most to divert people from God's wonderful plans for their lives, because deception very effectively leads them into temptation. So learning how to discern deception and guard against its evil lure is important.

The Free Online Dictionary defines deception this way: *To cause to believe what is not true; mislead; to give a false impression.* The dictionary further elaborates that deception *involves the deliberate misrepresentation of the truth: Mislead means to lead in the wrong direction or into error of thought or action.* We usually describe deceivers as being conniving, shrewd, devious, cunning, scheming, manipulative, or crafty.

Deception Leads to Bondage

The devil uses deception to lure us into temptation; if we yield to temptation, it will ensnare us in sin. The worst thing about deception is that its camouflage makes it difficult to detect. Quite often, we only find out that we have been deceived when we suffer the consequences.

> *The devil uses deception to lure us into temptation; if we yield to temptation, it will ensnare us in sin. The worst thing about deception is that its camouflage makes it difficult to detect.*

Judas is an example of a person who was ensnared by the spirit of deception. He was one of the appointed apostles of Jesus, yet he often stole money from the treasury bag. Perhaps he thought that all was well because he still continued to minister like the other apostles. Furthermore, maybe Jesus had never mentioned his sin; so Judas simply justified his actions. However, this self-deception led him further into the sin of greed to the point of betraying Jesus for money. He thought that he could get away with this sin as he had always done. However, things did not turn out the way he thought, and when he realized too late that he had been deceived, the damage was already done. What is even more unfortunate is that, instead of turning to God, he ended his own life.

Deception wants to enslave us; however, by seeking wisdom and the knowledge of God's Word, we can escape the snare of deception.

Deception Robs You

Deception is like a mirage that gives you a false illusion of your hopes. Satan deceived Adam and Eve into believing that they were going to be all-powerful and all-knowing like God. What they did not know was that falling into the trap of deception would cost far more than they thought they would gain. Deception never has your best interests at heart; it always comes with the sole agenda of robbing you.

> _Sharing your emotional wounds with a trusted friend or counselor will actually expose the deception of the devil and open the door for you to find healing._

Perhaps you are suffering from some emotional wounds that hurt you badly, but you hesitate to seek help because you fear being shunned and shamed. This kind of thinking is a deception intended to keep you enslaved to pain, and it will always rob your peace. Sharing your emotional wounds with a trusted friend or counselor will actually expose the deception of the devil and open the door for you to find healing.

Satan the Deceiver

Ultimately, all deception comes from the devil. The Bible calls him the father of lies (Read John 8:44); lying is his native language. He will lie to you about who you are, about your circumstances and options, and about your past, present, and future. The way to discern the lies of the devil is to measure every thought with the Word of God. If he says that you are unworthy, counteract that lie with the truth of God that you are fearfully and wonderfully made (Read Psalm 139:14).

The devil uses fear to intimidate us. The Bible says in 1 Peter 5:8, *Be self-controlled and alert. Your enemy the devil prowls around like a roaring lion looking for someone to devour.* Peter clearly states that the devil is not a lion; he only roars like a lion. He roars to deceive us into thinking that he is as ferocious as he sounds. If we yield to his intimidation, we will open a door for him to oppress us. The devil is not as strong as he pretends. The Bible says: *Greater is he that is in you than he that is in the world* (1 John 4:4). Also, *God hath not given us the spirit of fear; but of power, and of love, and of a sound mind* (2 Timothy 1:7). Therefore, with this truth we need to confront our fears boldly.

Signs of Deception

The story in Joshua 9:1-27 (please read this passage before proceeding) is an excellent example of how deception works. The Gibeonites have heard about how the Israelites conquered other nations, and they're terrified about facing the same fate. So they scheme to deceive the Israelites. Before the Israelites come to their land, the Gibeonites visit them and offer to make a covenant with them. They dress in worn-out clothes and carry moldy bread in order to deceive the Israelites into thinking that they've come from a far country. When Joshua inquires about their motives, they answer only some of his questions and then give other unnecessary information. They use evasion and overstatements to deceive Joshua. They sound convincing and persuasive. They spiritualize their answers and speak about things that they think would interest the Israelites. They even praise them to get them to let their guard down. Unfortunately, Joshua and the Israelites are deceived.

The Gibeonites clearly display the signs and traits of deception, some of which are exaggeration, shrewdness, disguised appearance, persuasive speech, evasive answers to questions, and hurrying decisions. Watch out for these signs of deception that lead to regrettable decisions.

Overcoming Deception

Because God is all-knowing, He can see beyond what you see. Learn to pray continually that the LORD will open your eyes to see deception. The Bible says in Matthew 7:7 (NIV), *Ask and it will be given to you; seek and you will find; knock and the door will be opened to you.* Just like King Solomon, ask God to give you a discerning heart of wisdom. God's wisdom will preserve and protect you from hidden snares. In order to discern deception, you need wisdom, knowledge, and understanding. And you can find these three elements in God's Word.

> *The worst thing about deception is that its camouflage makes it difficult to detect. Quite often, we only find out that we have been deceived when we suffer the consequences.*

The proverbs of Solomon son of David, king of Israel: for gaining wisdom and instruction; for understanding words of insight; for receiving instruction in prudent behavior, doing what is right and just and fair; for giving prudence to those who are simple, knowledge and discretion to the young— let the wise listen and add to their learning, let the discerning get guidance— for understanding proverbs and parables, the sayings and riddles of the wise.

Proverbs 1:1-6 (NIV)

In John 8:32 (NIV), Jesus said, *Then you will know the truth, and the truth will set you free.* Some kinds of bondage will break instantly when you know the truth. Truth not only reveals the deceit of the devil but also liberates you to walk in total freedom from fear. When you know you are forgiven and God loves you, you will not allow the deception that you are unworthy before God to hold you captive.

> *Seeking help from someone you trust who is not emotionally involved in your situation will help you identify signs of deception.*

When you are not sure which decision is the right one to make, you have to ask the right questions. Questions will quickly expose deception and provide clarity. Think about a con artist; he gets very uncomfortable when you begin to ask questions. In fact, a prosecutor in a courtroom will often cross-examine a suspect by asking questions in order to elicit this guilty response. In essence, questions reveal motives. So seek to know the pros and cons of each decision you make. Don't just look at short-term benefits; also look at the long-term benefits or consequences. Questions not only expose deception but also act like keys to unlock the truth.

Take time to make major decisions. Patience will eliminate the haste that can cost you dearly. But patience calls for delayed gratification. When your flesh wants something, it wants it now. Yielding to instant gratification keeps you from discerning the consequences of our decisions. Learn to practice patience in decision making, and patience will indeed reveal which decisions are bad ones.

Seeking help from someone you trust who is not emotionally involved in your situation will also help you identify signs of deception. When you focus on what deception has to offer, you will not see the consequences clearly. A trusted friend or counselor will see your blind spots and give you a broader perspective than you perceive alone. Remember: deception thrives most in isolation and secrecy; therefore, you can overcome it by sharing your intentions with the right people.

Chapter 7

Guard Against Toxic Relationships

When people speak about relationships, quite often they focus more on love relationships than other types. This chapter, however, will address relationships with people like friends and neighbors and coworkers. The kinds of friends we have influence our lives more than we think. In fact, they deeply mark our characters, values, decisions, and the direction of our lives. They will either build us or drain us. The Bible speaks profoundly on the influence of relationships.

Do not be misled: 'Bad company corrupts good character' (1 Corinthians 15:33).

The righteous choose their friends carefully (Proverbs 12:26).

One who has unreliable friends soon comes to ruin,
but there is a friend who sticks closer than a brother
(Proverbs 18:24).

Carefully choose the people you allow to influence you, because the negative influence that appeals to your carnal nature is more contagious than positive influence. Many people could significantly change their choices and attitudes for the better if they would only change their friends. Indeed, they would do well to follow the old saying: *If you cannot change your friends, change your friends.*

Types of Relationships

Parasitic Relationships

Parasitic relationships involve those people who have perfected the art of living off others. Parasites will befriend you because of what you have, not who you are. They are always needy and beset with problems. They nearly always call you about a problem they need you to solve for them. Their relationship with you works only one way. You're the giver, and they're the receiver. They view you as a service provider, and if you enable them, they will become even more demanding. Often such people do not want to work for what they need or walk the extra mile to get it. They strive to get what they want the easy way: living off others. They want others to do the hard work while they reap the benefits. The irony is that such people live off others not because they don't have the means to meet their needs but because they know they can easily get what they want from their friends.

Insecure Relationships

> *Another trait of domineering people is that they always want to be the center of attention. Conversations always center on them, what they have achieved, how they are better than others, etc.*

Insecure people have very negative mindsets. They always see the downside of anything good that another person does. They like to put other people down, and they do so intentionally to project themselves as better than others. If you have a friend who critiques everything you do or attempt to do, then you have an unhealthy relationship. Such people complain habitually about anything and everything, even when nothing is really wrong. Such friends drain your energy, motivation, and joy, because every time they talk to you they dampen your spirit with their negative venting. Such friends literally drain your spirit. They burden you and hinder your progress.

Domineering Relationships

Being the less powerful party in a domineering relationship is quite demeaning. Domineering people think that they are always right. As far as they are concerned, it is their way or no way; other people's ideas do not count. People who dominate their friends are intimidated by the success of others and tend to envy them. If you have friends who are very controlling, do not respect or value your opinions, or always want to make decisions for you, you need to end those friendships.

Another trait of domineering people is that they always want to be the center of attention. Conversations always center on them, what they have achieved, how they are better than others, etc. They tend to brag shamelessly. Such people never give you space to breathe. They want you to gain their approval for any decisions you make in your personal life. If you let them, they will run your life.

Manipulative Relationships

Some people like to manipulate their friends. Quite interestingly, manipulators are often friendly, giving, and outwardly quite compassionate; however, all these good qualities come with a price. Instead of giving freely, manipulators act sweetly to bribe you into doing them a very big favor. They take you on a guilt trip, recounting to you the many times they have helped you. They even play the victim, exaggerating their situation and shedding crocodile tears just to manipulate you into giving them what they want. They want to make you feel obligated to help. Such a relationship is very unhealthy; a manipulator only stays close to take advantage of you. The Bible says in Leviticus 25:17, *Do not take advantage of each other, but fear your God.*

> *An emotional affair occurs when a married person is emotionally tied to someone other than his or her spouse. Seeking emotional fulfillment from someone outside the marriage is not right, and it*

Abusive Relationships

If you feel insecure, fearful, and tense in a relationship, your feelings could be signs of an oppressive relationship that can easily turn abusive. Unfortunately, some people feel caged in abusive relationships. Many times, the victims in such circumstances are under the care of the abusers. They feel helpless and enslaved because they are dependent against their wishes. What even hurts more is that those who abuse them are people close to them who should be providing the love and tender care that they need.

Both verbal and physical abuse damage people emotionally. Abusers often threaten victims who talk to another person about the abuse. However, what victims need to know is that there is a way to freedom, and that way is through talking to someone. The threats also indicate that the abusers recognize that what they are doing is wrong, see the potential escape of the victims, and fear being caught. These reasons should give victims the courage to talk to someone, because the consequences of not telling anyone far outweigh the risks.

When the children of God faced insurmountable challenges, God reassured them. Deuteronomy 1:29-30 says, *"Then I said to you, 'Do not be terrified; do not be afraid of them. The LORD your God, who is going before you, will fight for you, as he did for you in Egypt."* Take heart! The LORD knows your pain, and He will give you grace and boldness when you speak to the right people about the abuse you are suffering.

Emotional Relationships

The term "emotional affair" might not be familiar to some, because it seems so harmless that people seldom address it as an unhealthy relationship. An emotional affair occurs when a married person is emotionally tied to someone other than his or her spouse. Seeking emotional fulfillment from someone outside the marriage is not right, and it leads to an unhealthy relationship.

> *As painful as separations are, the benefits far outweigh the losses. A healthy separation gives you an opportunity to find yourself after living in the shadow of someone else.*

People who feel emotionally disconnected from their spouses are vulnerable to emotional affairs. Lacking that emotional connection with their spouses, they may find another person of the opposite sex to meet their emotional needs. When this bond forms and they don't immediately disconnect, they will transfer more and more emotional ties to the sympathizer. Unfortunately, people involved in emotional affairs often don't feel guilty about them because there is no sex involved. However, emotional affairs often lead to a full-blown sexual affair. According to a MSNSC report, *About half of such emotional involvements do eventually turn into full-blown affairs, sex and all.* Infidelity researcher Shirley P. Glass also asserts that *82 percent of affairs happen with someone who was at first 'just a friend.'*

Not guarding against an emotional affair (even one that is not sexual), will adversely affect a marriage, further separating the couple. The Bible clearly states in Ephesians 5:3: *But among you there must not be even a hint of sexual immorality, or of any kind of impurity, or of greed, because these are improper for God's holy people.*

The key to guarding yourself against an emotional affair is learning to confront unresolved issues and investing the time to develop an honest and open relationship with your spouse. Depending upon your spouse as your source of emotional fulfillment will create a strong marriage bond and protect your relationship from outside threats. *Let marriage be held in honor (esteemed worthy, precious, of great price, and especially dear) in all things* (Hebrews 13:4 Amplified).

Relationship Solutions

The key to freedom is to end toxic relationships. You do not need to maintain relationships that are not adding value to your life. Of course, ending a relationship with people you have known for a long time is not easy, but it is necessary if you want to lead a more productive life. You may fear the consequences and pain of losing such relationships; however, the consequences of keeping them are far worse. Choosing to move on can be awkward, and you cannot avoid feeling the loss. However, do not cave to such feelings and retrieve that toxic relationship. Keep moving on and those awkward feelings will lessen with time.

> *"If you cannot change your friends, change your friends."*

As painful as separations are, the benefits far outweigh the losses. A healthy separation gives you an opportunity to find yourself after living in the shadow of someone else. It also provides you a chance to make choices that best suit you, not someone else. But even more importantly, a separation offers you the opportunity to pursue healthy relationships.

84

Just because you have lived with toxic relationships doesn't mean healthy relationships do not exist. You probably already know healthy and positive people who can influence you for the better. Maybe you wonder how a healthy relationship looks. It looks like being accepted for who you are, without anyone trying to change you to make you fit in. In a healthy relationship, you can be yourself. You can love and be loved.

Also, in a healthy relationship others care for you and act considerately. They respect you as a person, lovingly let you know when you are wrong, and help you to make right choices. In a healthy relationship, the give and take flows both ways. According to Scripture, relationships are supposed to be edifying. 1 Thessalonians 5:11 says, *Therefore encourage one another and build each other up, just as in fact you are doing.* When we pursue such relationships, they add value to us and bring the best out of us.

Chapter 8

Follow the Leading of God

Isaiah 30:21
Your ears shall hear a word behind you, saying,
"This is the way, walk in it,"
Whenever you turn to the right hand
Or whenever you turn to the left.

Natural Leading

God speaks to us in natural and supernatural ways. In the natural realm, He may give us inspired ideas, thoughts, knowledge, or wisdom concerning different aspects of our lives. Some people see using intellect or reasoning as carnal. However, God gave us a mind that reasons for a purpose. In fact, the Bible says, *For God has not given us a spirit of fear, but of power and of love and of a sound mind* (2 Timothy 1:7).

God gave King Solomon unique natural wisdom to govern the kingdom of Israel. *God gave Solomon wisdom and very great insight, and a breadth of understanding as measureless as the sand on the seashore. He spoke three thousand proverbs and his songs numbered a thousand and five. He described plant life, from the cedar of Lebanon to the hyssop that grows out of walls. He also taught about animals and birds, reptiles and fish* (1 Kings 4:29, 32-33 NIV).

> *Prophecy or divine revelation should never override Scripture. Regardless of what was said, who said it, or how mighty the supernatural experience felt, if the message does not agree with the Word of God, it is not from God.*

In the Bible, God sometimes told men specifically to do things that were contrary to human reasoning or cultural expectations. Some people may argue that we should never use our minds to reason. So how should we strike the balance? Because God gave us a mind that reasons, we should use it as He intended. Nevertheless, if He issues further divine instructions on how to deal with an issue that is beyond your reasoning, act by faith on His Word; you will see a supernatural manifestation.

God gave us five natural senses to help us in our daily living. However, they are only limited to the natural realm. The Spirit of God can guide us through situations that are beyond the abilities of our natural senses.

Supernatural Leading

The Bible gives many examples of God speaking to His people in supernatural ways, like visions, dreams, prophecies, and other divine experiences. Many people today testify that they have experienced the supernatural leading of God. Indeed, the LORD desires to lead us supernaturally. However, we have to be careful not to believe every supernatural manifestation as the leading of God. Unfortunately, some people have lived a nightmare that began when they followed a prophecy or supernatural manifestation that had not been tested. The challenge is not proving that God speaks through supernatural ways but testing whether what we heard or experienced came from Him. 1 John 4:1 states: _Beloved, do not believe every spirit, but test the spirits, whether they are of God; because many false prophets have gone out into the world._

Testing and Confirmation

Testing every prophecy or supernatural manifestation is imperative in seeking to know the will of God, because not all revelations or supernatural experiences are from the LORD. Some people think they are being disobedient and doubtful if they question a prophecy or supernatural directive, especially one that comes from a spiritual leader. Testing every word has nothing to do with disobedience or doubt; these considerations only apply when we know for sure that God has spoken to us.

Prophecy or divine revelation should never override Scripture. Regardless of what was said, who said it, or how mighty the supernatural experience felt, if the message does not agree with the Word of God, it is not from God. The LORD never contradicts His Word. The

Scriptures are superior to all else; they are the test of legitimacy. In fact, the Bible gives this stern warning, *If there arises among you a prophet or a dreamer of dreams, and he gives you a sign or a wonder, and the sign or the wonder comes to pass, of which he spoke to you, saying, 'Let us go after other gods' — which you have not known — 'and let us serve them,' you shall not listen to the words of that prophet or that dreamer of dreams* (Deuteronomy 13:1-3).

If you receive a prophecy that passes the scriptural test, the next step is to seek confirmation. Sometimes what is said may be biblically sound, but it may not be the word for you. You may receive a prophecy or dream that God has called you to be a missionary in another country; such a major decision needs confirmation, especially if God hasn't personally spoken to your heart about the matter before. If the message is from God, He will speak to your heart

> *In any given situation, once you establish that God is indeed leading you, have full confidence that He will fulfill His intended purpose in your life.*

and give you confirmation in many ways. And your search for confirmation should always begin with prayer to ask God for His guidance.

God can also give us confirmation through circumstances. In the above example, He can open doors and put in place all the details required for you to serve as a missionary. Confirmation also comes through the body of Christ, from other Christians who share the same conviction about the intuition you have in your heart, especially regarding your divine calling. People can easily see a genuine call of God in your life. Timing is also another indication of the Lord's confirmation. If you received a revelation that God was going to bless you with a specific thing, time will tell if indeed that revelation was from the LORD.

In the life of the apostle Paul, the Lord confirmed His Word on several occasions. *And see, now I go bound in the spirit to Jerusalem, not knowing the things that will happen to me there, except that the Holy Spirit testifies in every city, saying that chains and tribulations await me* (Acts 20:22-23).

Walking by Faith

In any given situation, once you establish that God is indeed leading you, have full confidence that He will fulfill His intended purpose in your life. Walk by faith, and you will see God's Word come to pass. Hebrews 11:1-2, 6 says, *Now faith is being sure of what we hope for and certain of what we do not see. This is what the ancients were commended for. . . And without faith it is impossible to please God, because anyone who comes to him must believe that he exists and that he rewards those who earnestly seek him* (NIV). When you willingly choose to follow the leading of God, expect great things to happen in your life.

Chapter 9

Choose God as Your Source of Fulfillment

The world defines success in terms of material things. It gauges success using the following three standards: knowledge, wealth, and influence. Society treats someone who achieves one or more of these standards with great respect and dignity. Many people pursue these standards at any cost, hoping to find acceptance, fulfillment, and self-worth. Choosing either or all of these elements as your source of fulfillment could lead to great disappointment.

The Vanity of Knowledge

Knowledge is an important part of life. Getting a good job without a good education is quite challenging to do anywhere in the world. In most job interviews, employers want to know your academic qualifications. In

> *In essence, the quantity of knowledge, wealth, or influence you have is not what determines fulfillment. You must know that neither the things of this world nor the things God can give will fulfill a man's life; only God HIMSELF can.*

fact, they use your level of education to gauge who can apply for a position. The more education you have, the greater your chances of getting a good job or climbing the corporate ladder.

Where would the world be were it not for the ingenious minds of the eighteenth and nineteenth centuries? We owe these men who introduced the industrial revolution to the world. They researched science and medicine and produced remarkable results. All these innovations stemmed from the quest for knowledge. Indeed, the search for knowledge has proved both fruitful and beneficial to our world. However, is knowledge our sole source of fulfillment and satisfaction?

Nehru, an Indian Prime Minister visiting America, once asked Albert Einstein, a famous American scientist, an interesting question. *Mr. Einstein, you have been called the greatest mind that ever lived; but have you discovered the purpose and meaning of life?*

Mr. Einstein bowed his head and softly replied, *No, I have not yet found the meaning of life.*

Isn't it amazing that a knowledgeable man like Einstein was still in search of the purpose and meaning of life?

The Vanity of Wealth

Imagine all the things you could do if you had more money. Life would be much easier and more comfortable. You would buy a bigger and better house, a new and luxurious car, dress the way you want, expand your business or ministry, and build a new state-of-the-art church building - the list goes on. Even the greatest critics of prosperity sermons would agree that we all could do with more money. After all, most people would like to live a better life!

As much comfort and luxury as wealth may provide, it is not the primary source of fulfillment in life. It is often said that *money is a good servant but a bad master.* You probably know people who own things that own them. The very things they bought to bring them comfort become harsh tyrants that rule every aspect of their lives. For example, someone who buys a vehicle or house that he can't afford may find the debt he owes controlling his budget, marriage, and family relations.

> *As much comfort and luxury as wealth may provide, it is not the primary source of fulfillment in life. It is often said that money is a good servant but a bad master.*

The assumption that life fulfillment is found in material things is such a misconception. Those who fall for this deception strive to accumulate more wealth only to long for more and more, and this vicious cycle never ends. In the Gospels, the rich young ruler asked Jesus a very pivotal question: *What good thing must I do to get eternal life?* Although he was wealthy, he still felt his life was lacking and sought to know what more he needed to do to have eternal life (Matthew 19:16-22).

One of the richest men in the world was asked, *How much is enough?*

His response was, *If only I could get a little bit more.*

His longing for more echoes Ecclesiastes 5:10: *Whoever loves money never has money enough; whoever loves wealth is never satisfied with his income.* Chuck Swindoll once said, *A good life only exists when one stops longing for another.*

The Vanity of Power and Influence

Since the time of Adam, man has always struggled with the quest for power and influence. God gave Adam the authority and dominion to rule over all His creation, but Adam still wasn't satisfied with the power that God had given him. The Bible states that Adam wanted to be like God, knowing good and evil. Deep down in his heart, Adam felt a quest for power and influence. Unfortunately, this quest led to his downfall.

The sons of Zebedee, James and John, were willing to pay any cost to get a position in God's kingdom. The mother of these two sons came to Jesus in an act of worship: *kneeling down, ask a favor of Him* (Matthew 20:20). She was willing to worship Christ in order to get her sons a position of influence. People go to great lengths in order to gain power and influence.

Having a position of influence sure feels great, more so because it comes with all the special benefits and privileges, but it can also be lonely. It is said that when Alexander the Great conquered the ancient world, he cried because there was no more land to conquer. Whether this tale is factual or not, one thing is for sure; the quest for power and influence is like trying to fill a leaking bucket with water. This thirst cannot be quenched.

In the book of Ecclesiastes, King Solomon wrote about his journey through life. He searched for meaning and fulfillment by experimenting with different pleasures and ideas. Although Solomon was the most knowledgeable, wealthy, and influential person of his time, he still tried different kinds of relationships in hopes of finding fulfillment. But even after marrying seven hundred wives and keeping a thousand concubines, Solomon could not fill the emptiness in his heart. At the end of his search for the meaning of life, Solomon concluded that the most fitting thing anyone can do is to *fear God and obey His commandments, for this is the whole duty of man* (Ecclesiastes 12:13 NIV).

> *Indeed, the search for knowledge has proved both fruitful and beneficial to our world. However, is knowledge our sole source of fulfillment and satisfaction?*

Discover the Source of Fulfillment

If knowledge, wealth, and influence are the actual sources of fulfillment in life, what happens to those individuals who do not have a college degree, who only earn minimum wage, or who are not considered to be influential people in their communities? Will they never find fulfillment? Unfortunately, many societies tend to despise such people and views them as failures, but how does God view them? Do they have any hope? On the other hand, what about the people who have succeeded materially and in their careers but still feel emptiness in their lives?

In essence, the quantity of knowledge, wealth, or influence you have is not what determines fulfillment. You must know that neither the things of this world nor the things God can give will fulfill a man's life; only God HIMSELF can. God is the source of fulfillment in life. When we seek Him first, the other things fall into place. *But seek first the kingdom of God and His righteousness, and all these things shall be added to you* (Matthew 6:33).

Indeed, the search for knowledge has proved both fruitful and beneficial to our world. However, is knowledge our sole source of fulfillment and satisfaction?

In the Bible, God used men and women from different walks of life to accomplish remarkable works. For instance, King Solomon was the wisest man who ever lived. On the other hand, the apostle Peter had little to no formal schooling. Nevertheless, God made him the lead apostle and also gave him divine wisdom to establish the early church. Consider David, who was successful and wealthy. He left a legacy that impacted many lives. On the other hand, the poor widow mentioned the New Testament gave only a mite. However, Jesus spoke highly of her generosity. Think about Daniel, a high-ranking government official who spiritually influenced the kings of Babylon. As for Amos, he was just a shepherd that God used as a prophet to the nation of Israel.

What did all these people have in common? They pursued an intimate relationship with God, even though some stumbled along the way. Nevertheless, through their mistakes and wrong choices, they learned that neither the things of this world nor the things God could give them would fulfill their lives. They finally realized that the real source of fulfillment in life is God alone. David asked the LORD to grant his greatest desire, which was to dwell in the house of God all the days of his life (Read Psalm 27:4). He could have asked for knowledge, wealth, or influence, but he chose God, who would satisfy the desires of his heart. Like David, choose God as your source of fulfillment, and then you will find meaning in life.

Chapter 10

Choose God's Best for Your Life

Have you ever taken a journey of faith in what you knew for sure was God's leading? Everything seemed clear when you received God's directives; you had no doubt that God was on your side and that He would fulfill every promise He gave you. But after what you thought would take days or perhaps a few weeks to be fulfilled turned into months and years of waiting, you started doubting. Time seemed to be running out, and your outward circumstances seemed to contradict the promise. What began as a bright light of hope slowly faded as you faced the odds against you. In such a situation, natural reasoning would surely suggest that you seek an alternative, logical option in the natural world rather than clinging to hope in the supernatural world.

Abraham was in just such a predicament. When Abraham was seventy-five, the LORD promised him that he would father a great nation of his own offspring. Abraham obeyed God and took this journey of faith. After ten years of walking in faith, he still saw no sign of the promised son. Faced with the limitations of age, Abraham and Sarah opted to bear a child through Hagar, a bondservant of Sarah. Unfortunately, the couple did not fully consider the consequences of bearing the son of presumption, Ishmael, instead of waiting for the son of promise, Isaac.

Sometimes when the LORD takes too long to fulfill His promises, we tend to think that an Ishmael option is better than persevering through a season of barrenness. Even though an Ishmael option may seem to be a reasonable substitute for the promised Isaac, troubling consequences come from acting without God. Through the story of Abraham, we discover four reasons why people choose Ishmael over Isaac.

Whenever you take steps of faith to follow the promises God has given you, you need to remember that God fulfills His promises within His timeline, not yours.

The Timing Seems Too Late

When the LORD gave Him the promise of a son, Abraham was not a sprightly lad with a barren young bride. He and Sarah were old enough to be grandparents, and Sarah's time of bearing children was long gone. Having lost all hope, Abraham and Sarah opted to have Ishmael. Although God told them clearly that Ishmael was not the promised son and that He would bless them with Isaac, Abraham still doubted the LORD, saying, *Will a son be born to a man of a hundred years*

old? Will Sarai bear a child at the age of ninety? ...If only
Ishmael might live under the blessing* (Genesis 17:17-18).

Sometimes out of despair, we ask the LORD to
bless the options we attempt alone rather than continue
believing God for His promise. Perhaps God led you to
start a business or ministry, but the business or ministry
has been struggling to succeed. Although you know that
God began this work, getting a job or serving in another
ministry and trusting God to bless it just as He would
have blessed what He began seems easier. Do not give up
on the promise of God. Keep in mind that your Ishmael
option is not God's best for you.

Whenever you take steps of faith to follow the
promises God has given you, you need to remember that
God fulfills His promises within His timeline, not yours.
We should still set goals and plan for the future, but our
goals and plans should move us toward the promises of
God as we trust Him to fulfill them in His time. The
problem with working independently from our own timing
is that we set ourselves up for disappointment when our
deadlines do not meet our expectations. When that
disappointment comes, many people walk away from the
promises of God.

For us to overcome this hurdle, we need to know a
couple of things about God's timing. First, God knows
when the time is right for your Isaac to be born. The irony
is that, because He does not use the natural course of
events to determine the right time of fulfillment, He will
sometimes arrive with promise in hand when we least
expect Him. The book of Genesis records that Isaac
planted crops in the year of a famine and reaped a
hundred-fold (Genesis 26:1, 12). The Bible also says, *He
[God] has made everything beautiful in its time*

(Ecclesiastes 3:11). God knows your season better than you do.

The second thing about the timing of God is that time does not limit Him. God is the one who controls time. He can change things as He pleases. When Joshua needed more time to fight his enemies, the LORD moved the time back by twelve hours (Joshua 10:12-13). If He has the ability to control time, why should you worry about running out of time? So do not interpret any delays of God's promises as denials. God is never early or late. He comes right on time.

> *The fact that everyone else doubted Paul's conviction did not change or affect the fulfillment of God's Word. The opposition or majority opinion of others does not indicate that their choice is God's will.*

The third thing about the timing of God is that the LORD has to prepare you for the blessing. If you were to receive the blessing before the appointed time, you would lose it. The prodigal son thought he was ready to handle his inheritance, but time proved that he was not ready to handle this huge responsibility. Because of his immaturity, he lost all his inheritance. When he went back to his father, he asked him to make him like one of his servants (Luke 15:11-21). Although the prodigal felt unworthy to be called a son in his father's household, he also realized that he needed to learn how to be responsible as a servant before being entrusted again with his father's wealth.

Have you settled for an Ishmael option because God's promise to you has taken too long? You may want to reconsider the Isaac promise, even though it seems to take too long. The Bible says, *For the vision is yet for an appointed time; but at the end it will speak, and it will not lie. Though it tarries, wait for it; because it will surely come, it will not tarry* (Habakkuk 2:3).

Your Inward Intuition Conflicts with Your Outward Circumstances

Sometimes walking by faith feels like walking on a tightrope between two ten-story buildings that are fifty feet apart. You're holding only a skinny pole to keep your balance, knowing very well that any miscalculated step would end your life. Attempting such a stunt can only lead to success or total disaster.

Think of Peter, who had an inward intuition to walk on water, yet the outward storms and winds challenged his faith. Although he started sinking at some point, at least he experienced the miracle of walking on water. How many people fear to attempt great things for God because they might fail? You will never know what you can accomplish until you take a risk. When you feel doubt creeping in like Peter did, call on Jesus. He will strengthen your faith.

As long as you know that the intuition in your heart is from God, you should not fear the outward circumstances. God does not depend on your outward circumstances to fulfill His promise in your life, but on your faith. The Bible states that *faith is the substance of things hoped for, the evidence of things not seen* (Hebrews 11:1). Faith looks beyond the outward circumstances to believe that God will fulfill His promises.

Others Doubt Your Convictions

Sticking to your convictions is not always easy to do when others doubt them. In the case of Abraham, Sarah was not convinced that God wanted her to have a baby at her old age. She tried to interpret God's promise in her own way to suit her lack of faith. People will try to talk you out of God's promises based on their carnal reasoning. I have come to understand that I cannot walk in another man's revelation, just as no one else can walk in mine. People will not always see what God has shown you unless He reveals it to them. So having a different perspective from others is common.

> *God's promises for your life are subject to obedience. We must be willing to walk in obedience if we want to see God fulfill His promises in our lives.*

When the apostle Paul was sailing to Italy for his trial, the LORD told him that the ship would face a storm that would destroy it, but all souls aboard would be saved. When he shared this revelation with the sailors, they ignored him. After all, how could a criminal on death row have anything worthwhile to say? The fact that everyone else doubted Paul's conviction did not change or affect the fulfillment of God's Word. The opposition or majority opinion of others does not indicate that their choice is God's will. When all Israel cried out for a king to be like other nations, the prophet Samuel was convinced that Jehovah was enough to be the one and only true king of Israel.

When others doubt your convictions, do not ignore godly counsel to appease them. The Bible says, _But in the multitude of counselors there is safety_ (Proverbs 11:14b). Seek people who will give you godly counsel, not those who want to make decisions for you. People who give godly counsel do not talk you out of your convictions. Rather, they give you information to help you make wise decisions.

> When others doubt your convictions, do not ignore godly counsel to appease them. The Bible says, But in the multitude of counselors there is safety (Proverbs 11:14b).

Going against the Flow Seems to Be the Wrong Direction

Going against the flow takes great faith and courage. Going with the flow is always easier; anyone can do it. After all, even a dead fish can go downstream. The Bible says, _Enter by the narrow gate; for wide is the gate and broad is the way that leads to destruction, and there are many who go in by it. Because narrow is the gate and difficult is the way which leads to life, and there are few who find it_ (Matthew 7:13-14).

Not everyone is willing to pay the price of following God and staying committed to His Word. If anything, many people would rather go through the broad gate, which is convenient and allows them to carry whatever they wish. But the narrow gate that leads to life demands that we deny ourselves some things and friends that we treasure dearly.

Choosing to go against the flow is uncomfortable, and it also leads to criticism and ridicule. However, no man can do anything outstanding unless he stands out of the ordinary. Doing the extraordinary requires going against the flow. God's promises for your life often go against the flow of your situation. Moses was not eloquent in speech when God called him to be His mouthpiece. Gideon felt inferior when God called him to do the superior. Sarah was aged and barren when the LORD promised her a son. All these people had to go against the flow in order to realize God's promise for them.

> *Sometimes when the LORD takes too long to fulfill His promises, we tend to think that an Ishmael option is better than persevering through a season of barrenness. Even though an Ishmael option may seem to be a reasonable substitute for the promised Isaac, troubling consequences come from acting without God.*

Consequences of an Ishmael Option

Nothing else is as sad as realizing that you had a better option, especially when you see the success of those who patiently waited on God. An Ishmael option may offer short-term solutions. Nonetheless, it has long-term consequences. When we take this option, we sacrifice the valuable for what is less valuable and the significant for the insignificant.

Although God gave Abraham Isaac in the end, Abraham still had to deal with the estranged relationship between Sarah and Hagar. Worse still, Abraham's mistake created a family feud between the households of Isaac and Ishmael that lasted many generations. When Isaac was still a child, Ishmael mocked him (Genesis 21:8-9). Generations later, Ishmaelite slave traders sold Isaac's descendant Joseph as a slave in Egypt. Today the Muslims in Palestine who claim Abraham as their father through Ishmael still fight against Jews who also claim Abraham as their father through Isaac.

An Ishmael option will always cost you more that you think. It may become a snare to your blessing.

> _Choosing to go against the flow is uncomfortable, and it also leads to criticism and ridicule._
> _However, no man can do anything outstanding unless he stands out of the ordinary._

Trust God for Your Promise

God's promises for your life are subject to obedience. We must be willing to walk in obedience if we want to see God fulfill His promises in our lives. Deuteronomy 28 lists the blessings that would follow the Israelites if they obeyed God and the curses that would befall them if they disobeyed. As Christians, we have to remember that fulfilling the promises of God it is not all up to God; He expects us to submit to Him. Another thing to note is that not all the promises of God arrive without a battle or an obligation. Many times people think that when the LORD gives them a promise, all they have to do is sit and wait for it.

The Lord promised the Israelites a land flowing with milk and honey where they would inherit houses they did not build and vineyards they did not plant. But have you ever considered that they had to fight the giants of the land before possessing it? In Joshua 1:8, the LORD gave the Israelites the strategy of winning the battle over the giants so that they could possess the Promised Land. *This Book of the Law shall not depart from your mouth, but you shall meditate in it day and night, that you may observe to do according to all that is written in it. For then you will make your way prosperous, and then you will have good success.*

We can learn from Abraham that even though we may have made a wrong choice at one point or another, God is gracious enough to give us a second chance. We can learn from our past mistakes and use them as stepping stones to trusting God like never before. So when Ishmael seems to be an option, just consider the long-term consequences, and wait for your Isaac, no matter how long God takes to fulfill the promise, because His blessings are wonderful and worthwhile.

Chapter 11

Embrace God's Plan for Your Life

God reveals His plan for our lives partially by the wonderful and unique qualities He places in us. We understand very well that man invents his every innovation to perform specific functions. Think of all the appliances, equipment, and machines we use daily. Their makers design them differently in order to perform various tasks. In the same manner, God creates each of us to pursue a specific course in life. He places diverse gifts, talents, skills, and passions in us to accomplish the work He assigns to us. The Bible says, *As each one has received a gift, minister it to one*

> *Fear of allowing God to guide your life will always keep you from knowing the great things you can accomplish with Him.*

another, as good stewards of the manifold grace of God (1 Peter 4:10). God has a plan for your life that He had in mind when He created you. Embrace His plan, and it will fulfill and delight you.

Why People Don't Follow God's Plan

If God has such wonderful plans for our lives, why do we sometimes struggle with embracing His plans? Proverbs 19:21 reveals our tug of war between our plans and God's plan for us. *Many are the plans in a man's heart, but it is the LORD's purpose that prevails* (NIV). The following seven reasons describe why people struggle to follow God's plan for their lives.

They Do Not Walk by Faith

Perhaps the most challenging thing about following God's plan for your life is walking by faith, not by sight. When you follow your plan, you figure everything out. You know all the details. You know how the plan will unfold. However, following God's plan requires total dependence on Him. This kind of reliance grates against your self-driven will. Handing control of your life to someone else is the last thing you want. Often as you follow God's plan for your life, He will lead you through unfamiliar territory, rough terrain, and dark alleys. He will take you south when He told you that the destination lies north. Following God requires total faith in Him. *For we walk by faith, not by sight* (2 Corinthians 5:7).

They Do Not Believe That the Destination Is Worth the Trouble

Because the experiences of the journey can challenge us, sometimes we wonder whether God's plan is worth following. The children of Israel were in such a predicament. They left Egypt with great excitement. They were going to a land flowing with milk and honey. Although the trials they faced along the way caused many of them to lose hope in the promise, God desired to lead them every step of the way.

Without this knowledge, we feel left alone in a giant maze to figure out the way to our destiny. Throughout the journey from Egypt to Canaan, the LORD provided a cloud by day and pillar of fire by night to guide the Israelites. In the same way, His Spirit is with us today to guide us through the journey. Jesus gave us this promise: *It is to your advantage that I go away; for if I do not go away, the Helper [Holy Spirit] will not come to you; but if I depart, I will send Him to you* (John 15:7).

They Do Not Totally Trust in God

Although you may be fully aware that God has a wonderful plan for your life, your lack of trust during trying times can keep you from pursuing God's plan. Following God's plan for your life requires you to trust Him even during moments of uncertainty, because He is well able to carry you through safely. *Every word of God is pure; He is a shield to those who put their trust in Him* (Proverbs 30:5). Remember that He has the bird's eye view of the maze and can easily see the path to your destiny. If only you can learn to let God have full control, you can enjoy the ride after all. When you travel by plane, you entrust your life to a human pilot you have never met. Even though you have no idea how to fly a plane, you have full confidence that the pilot knows what he is doing.

They Fear Losing Control

Some people often perceive the will of God to be confusing and cumbersome. So they think that if they yield to it, their lives will be out of control. Some fear that if they yield to God's will, He will ask them to do the very thing they hate to do. They think that God will ask them to give up everything, go to unfamiliar places, and live miserable lives. They assume quite wrongly that God wants to frustrate them in every way.

Fear of allowing God to guide your life will always keep you from knowing the great things you can accomplish with Him. It can also cause you to doubt God who knows you completely and wants to help you. *A man's steps are directed by the LORD. How then can anyone understand his own way?* (Proverbs 20:24 NIV).

They Lack Knowledge of God's Plan

Some people are simply unaware that God has a divine plan for their lives; so they never seek God's plan. For one to struggle painfully through life when help is within reach is quite a sad fate. Tragically, a man in Michigan froze to death in his house because his utility bill of about a thousand dollars went unpaid. What was even more saddening was that the man had over six hundred thousand dollars in his savings account. Could we sometimes lack only because we either don't know or we don't ask?

Yet you do not have because

> *For there is a proper time and procedure for every matter, though a man's misery weighs heavily upon him*
>
> Ecclesiastes 8:6 (NIV)

113

you do not ask. You ask and do not receive, because you ask amiss (James 4:2-3).

They Don't Understand God's Ways

When the Bible talks about God's ways, it means His directives, methods, order, approach, or procedure. The Bible says, *'For my thoughts are not your thoughts, neither are your ways my ways,'* declares the LORD. *'As the heavens are higher than the earth, so are my ways higher than your ways and my thoughts than your thoughts'* (Isaiah 55:8-9 NIV). God wants us to take a specific way to fulfill His will for our lives. Often when we catch a glimpse of what He has called us to do, we excitedly begin to do it our way without considering how He wants the job done. This presumption often causes us conflict within that grows when we hit a dead end or fail in our endeavor to do God's will.

> *Knowing that God's plans for us are not only good and pleasing, but also fault-free is very empowering. Although we make mistakes, God never makes mistakes in His plans.*

David had such an encounter (2 Samuel 6). The first time he tried to retrieve the Ark of the Covenant, he failed, and a man died. David wondered why he hadn't succeeded, even though he knew that the will of God was for him to restore the Ark of the Covenant to Jerusalem. When David sought God, he found the LORD's specific instructions detailing how the Ark of the Covenant must be carried. In the first attempt, David created his own guidelines. But the second time, he sought God's direction: *For there is a proper time and procedure for every matter, though a man's misery weighs heavily upon him* (Ecclesiastes 8:6 NIV).

They Do Not Understand God's Thoughts

When the Bible talks about God's thoughts, it means His plans, purposes, objectives, reasons, intent, ideals, or course. God's thoughts are quite different from ours. The Bible says, *No eye has seen, no ear has heard, no mind has conceived what God has prepared for those who love him — but God has revealed it to us by his Spirit. The Spirit searches all things, even the deep things of God . . . In the same way no one knows the thoughts of God except the Spirit of God. We have not received the spirit of the world but the Spirit who is from God, that we may understand what God has freely given us. 'For who has known the mind of the Lord that he may instruct him?' But we have the mind of Christ* (1 Corinthians 2:10-16 NIV).

As the above scripture states, the LORD wants to reveal His thoughts and plans to us. He does so through His Spirit, who knows His mind and gives us the wonderful revelation of God's plans.

The Blessings of Following God's Plan

His Plans Are Easier to Follow than Ours

Take my yoke upon you and learn from me, for I am gentle and humble in heart, and you will find rest for your souls. For my yoke is easy and my burden is light (Matthew 11:29-30 NIV).

The fact that we do not fully know God's plans for our lives doesn't mean they are burdensome. In fact, His plans are a whole lot easier to follow than ours. Why struggle with your own plans when God's plans for you are good and quite achievable?

His Plans are Good, Pleasing, and Perfect

Do not conform any longer to the pattern of this world, but be transformed by the renewing of your mind. Then you will be able to test and approve what God's will is — his good, pleasing and perfect will (Romans 12:2 NIV).

Knowing that God's plans for us are not only good and pleasing, but also fault-free is very empowering. Although we make mistakes, God never makes mistakes in His plans. This guarantee is our assurance when we pursue His plans for us. The LORD promised Joshua, _Observe to do according to all the law which Moses My servant commanded you; do not turn from it to the right hand or to the left, that you may prosper wherever you go_ (Joshua 1:7).

His Plans Prevail over Human Limitations

So he said to me, "This is the word of the LORD to Zerubbabel: 'Not by might nor by power, but by my Spirit,' says the LORD Almighty" (Zechariah 4:6 NIV).

Your human abilities limit your plans, but God's plans for your life go beyond your human abilities. His purposes prevail over all your human limitations.

> _Often as you follow God's plan for your life, He will lead you through unfamiliar territory, rough terrain, and dark alleys. He will take you south when He told you that the destination lies north. Following God requires total faith in Him. For we walk by faith, not by sight (2 Corinthians_

116

Follow His plans, and you will see His power at work overcoming the obstacles that you face. His unlimited power will demolish any stumbling blocks that arise to keep you from fulfilling your divine purpose.

His Plans Are Prosperous and Filled with Hope

For I know the plans I have for you," declares the LORD, "plans to prosper you and not to harm you, plans to give you hope and a future (Jeremiah 29:11 NIV).

We live in an uncertain world. However, in God we have a sure hope for a blessed and prosperous future. Even when the storms of life confront us, God will either calm the storms or calm our hearts in the midst of the storm and lead us safely to our destination. The apostle Paul survived a shipwreck on his journey to Rome; the LORD delivered everyone on board and used that situation to allow Paul to preach the gospel (Acts 27).

His Plans Bring Great Joy

Great is my boldness of speech toward you, great is my boasting on your behalf. I am filled with comfort. I am exceedingly joyful in all our tribulation (2 Corinthians 7:4).

No greater joy in life exists than to fulfill God's will for you. Even in the midst of trials and difficult times, the LORD will fill your heart with joy. You will become a great testimony for those around you when they realize that your situation does not determine your joy: God does.

His Plans Completely Satisfy

The fear of the LORD leads to life, and he who has it will abide in satisfaction; he will not be visited with evil (Proverbs 19:23).

117

When we fulfill the will of God, we will find great satisfaction in knowing that we are doing what we were born to do. Our divine purpose is the only reason why we exist; therefore, when we fulfill our life's purpose, great satisfaction fills our hearts.

His Plans Impact the World

But the people who know their God shall be strong, and carry out great exploits (Daniel 11:32).

If you desire to make a difference in the world, allow the LORD to work in you and through you. His plans for your life go beyond meeting your needs; He wants to use you to bless others.

> *Inside the will of God there is no failure; outside the will of God there is no success* (Bernard Edinger).

His Plans Succeed

Uzziah did what was right in the eyes of the LORD, just as his father Amaziah had done. He sought God during the days of Zechariah, who instructed him in the fear of God. As long as he sought the LORD, God gave him success (2 Chronicles 26:4-5 NIV).

The following quote says it well: *Inside the will of God there is no failure; outside the will of God there is no success* (Bernard Edinger). Following God's plan for your life is the key to ultimate success.

118

Chapter 12

Make the Ultimate Choice

Before the State of Ohio ban on public smoking, waiters in restaurants frequently asked customers whether they preferred smoking or non-smoking seating. In regards to salvation, people too often perceive it as a fire insurance policy against hell. Perhaps ministers and evangelists far too often present the message of salvation as an option between smoking (hell) and non-smoking (heaven). Although Scripture clearly states the implications of our eternal choices, eternal life is much more than just a destination; it's an intimate relationship with God.

In the beginning, Adam had just such a wonderful, loving, and personal relationship with God. In fact, because of that strong bond, the LORD entrusted His entire creation on earth to Adam and blessed Adam and Eve with the beautiful Garden of Eden as their home.

They lived a blissful life in the abundance of God's blessings, provision, and protection. However, because of their greed (they wanted to be all-knowing and powerful like God) they ate the fruit God had placed off-limits. Their sin broke their wonderful relationship with God, separating them from Him. Adam's greed blinded him from realizing that he was exchanging the blessings of God for a curse and the kingship of God for the reign of Satan. *And even if our gospel is veiled, it is veiled to those who are perishing. The god of this age has blinded the minds of unbelievers, so that they cannot see the light of the gospel of the glory of Christ, who is the image of God* (2 Corinthians 4:3-4 NIV). Adam's own choice led him to live in a world ruled by Satan and filled with hate, crime, rebellion, and all kinds of evil.

Although the curse of sin and death entered the world through Adam, God still had a wonderful plan through Christ to reconcile this broken relationship with humans. *Therefore, just as sin entered the world through one man, and death through sin, and in this way death came to all men, because all sinned . . . But the gift is not like the trespass. For if the many died by the trespass of the one man, how much more did God's grace and the gift that came by the grace of the one man, Jesus Christ, overflow to the many . . . For just as through the disobedience of the one man the many were made sinners, so also through the obedience of the one man the many will be made righteous* (Romans 5:12, 15, 19).

> *Therefore, just as sin entered the world through one man, and death through sin, and in this way death came to all men, because all sinned.*
>
> Romans 5:12

God plans not only redeem mankind from the eternal death caused by sin but also to grant them abundant life. Jesus said, _I have come that they may have life, and that they may have it more abundantly_ (John 10:10). Even though we still live in a fallen world full of trials and challenges, our new life in Christ is a great and fulfilling gift that is worth accepting even in difficulty. This new life does not begin when we die and go to heaven; it begins when we choose to commit our lives to God.

Once I heard a story told by Evangelist Reinhard Bonnke of an old wise man who mesmerized the people of his town with his great wisdom so that people came from far and wide to seek his counsel. One day, a young boy came to him intending to prove the man wrong. With a butterfly clenched in his hand, the boy asked the old man whether the insect was dead or alive. If the old man said the butterfly was dead, the boy planned to release it to fly. But if he said it was alive, he would squeeze it to death. When he asked the wise man whether the butterfly was dead or alive, the old man pondered the question and then said, "It all depends on you."

Experiencing the abundant life God promised also depends on us. Making the ultimate choice of accepting Christ's gift of salvation will completely transform your life. This choice is the first step in the wonderful journey of fulfilling the great plans God has for your life.

> Jesus said, _I have come that they may have life, and that they may have it more abundantly._
>
> John 10:10

Take Action

To accept Jesus Christ as your Lord and savior today, pray the following simple prayer. This prayer does not save you; however, your faith and confession to God does, Romans 10:8-10 *But what does it say? "The word is near you, in your mouth and in your heart"[a] (that is, the word of faith which we preach): 9 that if you confess with your mouth the Lord Jesus and believe in your heart that God has raised Him from the dead, you will be saved. 10 For with the heart one believes unto righteousness, and with the mouth confession is made unto salvation.* This prayer is just a guide to help you make this confession.

Dear God,

I acknowledge that I am a sinner, and I do not have a right relationship with You. I repent of my sins and ask You to forgive me. I believe that You died on the cross for me, to save me. You did what I could not do for myself. I come to You now and ask You to become the Savior and LORD of my life. Help me to live every day in a way that pleases You. I love You, LORD, and I thank You that I will spend all eternity with You. Amen!

Congratulations! You have just made the most important decision of your life. You are now a born-again Christian, and your wonderful journey with the LORD has just begun. The great news is that the LORD wants to walk with you throughout this journey. He will help you when you stumble, in moments of doubt, during tough times, and in every season in your life. Write to us today at information@vesselofhonor.org and let us know about your decision to follow Christ. We will be very glad to give you more information on how to grow spiritually. We look forward hearing from you.

May the Lord bless you!

Boniface G. Gitau

STUDY GUIDE
Lessons

Wise Choices Life Application

Lesson One

Peer Pressure

1. What is peer pressure?

2. Identify and discuss areas people experience peer pressure.

3. Write reasons why people yield to peer pressure.

4. List some of the consequences of yielding to peer pressure.

5. How can one overcome peer pressure? Read Proverbs 18:24, Proverbs 13:20 & Psalm 1:1-3

6. Read 1 Kings 12:1-20. From the account of King Rehoboam what lessons can we learn about peer pressure?

7. Rather than yielding to peer pressure, discuss ways we can positively influence our peers.

8. List three steps you will take to guard against yielding to peer pressure when making right decisions.

Prayer Guide

Ask God for the boldness to make right decisions when faced with peer pressure.

Wise Choices Life Application

Lesson Two

Instant Gratification

1. What comes to mind when you hear the words 'instant gratifications?'

2. Discuss reasons why instant gratification is so tempting.

3. From the story of Adam and Eve why will instant gratification cost one in the long run? Read Genesis 3:1-20

4. The antidote for instant gratification is patience/delayed gratification. What can we learn about patience in the following verses:

   a. Hebrews 6:12

   b. James 5:7-11

   c. Psalm 40:1

5. Joseph resisted temptations and endured through his trial in Egypt. Discus some of the fruits and benefits of patience and endurance? Read Romans 5:3-5 and Psalm 105:16-24

6. Write three things you will do to guard yourself from yielding to instant gratifications.

Wise Choices Life Application

Lesson Three

Emotions and Decisions

1. Discuss why God gave us emotions?

2. Can our emotions be trusted in decision making? Discuss

3. How should we respond to our emotions when making decisions?

4. Read Proverbs 15:1 and discuss how reacting to emotions like anger can affect our judgment in decision making.

5. Since making decisions based on emotions alone could lead to dire consequence; what can we do to put our emotions in check while making decisions? Review chapter one, page 24 - 27.

6. Emotions are often expressed through desires, what can be learn from Galatians 5:13-26

7. Sometimes doing the right things doesn't always feel good. Identify five wise decisions you need to make even though you don't feel like it and list steps you will take to do them.

Prayer Guide

Ask God to help you learn to make the right decisions regardless of your feelings.

Wise Choices Life Application

Lesson Four

Admitting Mistakes

1. Is admitting one's mistake a strength or a weakness? Discuss

2. Why do people struggle with admitting their sins or mistakes?

3. Discuss the consequences of not admitting one's mistakes

4. Read Psalm 51. In the account of David and Bethsebath discuss lessons learnt from how David dealt with his sin

5. What positive things can come out of admitting one's mistakes?

6. How can one gather courage to admit his/her mistakes? Read Hebrews 4:15-16

7. Admitting our mistake is a great step to taking responsibility, however, what other steps do we need to amend our mistakes? Read Ephesians 4:22-24

Prayer Guide

Pray for humility of heart so as to learn admitting and amending our mistakes. Ask God for the knowledge and wisdom to learn from those mistakes.

Wise Choices Life Application

Lesson Five

Accepting Forgiveness

1. Why do people sometimes struggle with forgiving themselves and accepting God's forgiveness?

2. According to your perspective describe God's forgiveness

3. How can we describe God's love and forgiveness according to the following scriptures?
    a. Isaiah 53:1-12

b. John 3:16

c. 1 John 3:1

4. Read Romans 8:1 and John 8:1-11. From the story the woman caught in the act of adultery what is the difference between condemnation and conviction?

5. What can we learn about God's forgiveness according to 1 John 1:9?

6. Identify areas in your life where you struggle to forgive yourself and others.

7. Read the following scriptures and write specific actions you will take in relation to forgiving yourself and others.

   a) 1 John 1:9

   b) Ephesians 1:7

   c) Colossians 2:13

d) Matthew 18:21-35

e) Mark 11:25

f) Matthew 6:14-15

Prayer Guidance

Ask God to give you grace to accept His forgiveness and to forgive yourself and others.

Wise Choices Life Application

Lesson Six

Confronting False Guilt

1. What is the definition of false guilt? Refer to chapter 3.

2. Where does false guilt come from? Read Revelation 12:10

3. Signs of false guilt – Discuss some of the commons accusations satan brings on believers.

4. Read Revelation 12:9-1 and John 10:10. The bible exposes satan's agenda; what can we learn from these scriptures about dealing with satan's weapon of false guilt?

5. According to Hebrews 10:19-23 (NIV) what confidence can we have when dealing with satan's accusations that bring false guilt?

6. What confidence can we have in God? Read

   a. Hebrews 10:19-22

b. Romans 3:25-27

7. Identify areas in your life where you struggle with false
   guilt. Based on the scriptures you've read in this
   lesson how should you respond to false guilt?

Prayer Guidance

*In Christ we can find peace and freedom when we ask for
his forgiveness. Ask the LORD for the wisdom to identify
and deal with false guilt.*

Wise Choices Life Application

Lesson Seven

Confronting Rejection

1. Does Jesus identify with us when we experience rejection? Read Isaiah 53:1-3 and Matthew 27:32-46

2. Discuss causes of rejection

3. What are some of the results of allowing feelings of rejection?

4. How does rejection affect our relationship with God?

5. People who suffer from rejection tend to isolate themselves from others; what are the dangers of isolation? Read 1 Kings 19:1-1

6. According to the following scriptures how can we overcome rejection and isolation?

    a. Joshua 1:5

    b. Hebrews 10:25

    c. Proverbs 18:24

Prayer Guidance

God accepts us on the basis of His love and not our good works. Pray that the LORD will help you learn to trust in His promise that "He will never leave you nor forsake you."

Wise Choices Life Application

Lesson Eight

Overcoming Fear

1. When dealing with fear it is important to know that fear does not come from God. Read Romans 8:15 and 2 Timothy 1:7 and write what the LORD says about fear.

2. It is normal for us to feel fearful and anxious when we are vulnerable however, how we respond to fear is more important than how we feel. Discuss and list some of the common fears we often face.

3. It is possible for us to overcome our fear. Read 1 Samuel 17:1-58, then compare and contrast David and the army of Israel.

a. What caused the Saul's army to fret even though each man had weapons and armor?

b. What gave David the courage to face a giant warrior who was experienced, had a shield bearer, and superior weapons?

4. Fear is often a result of lack of trust in God. In fact it reveals our self-trust and self-reliance. Read the following scriptures and discuss how you can apply them.

a. Proverbs 3:5-6

b. John 14:27

c. Psalm 23

d. Psalm 34:4

5. List the four steps stated in Philippians 4:6-7 on how to deal with anxiety (fear). Also state the results they will produce.

Prayer Guidance

Pray for courage to confront fear and anxiety.

Wise Choices Life Application

Lesson Nine

Triumph Over Lies We Believe

1. Who we believe we are is largely influenced by what others said about us while growing up. Compare and contrast the following:

   a. What others say about me

   b. Who I believe I am

2. Based on the response on question one is there a co-relation between how others value us and how we value ourselves? Discuss

3. Perhaps before we go any further discuss the definition of self-worthy.

4. Do others or our heritage, ethnicity, background or past experiences really determine our self-worth? Read Judges 6:11-16 and compare and contrast how Gideon viewed himself and how God viewed him. List your findings.

5. Where should our self-worth come from? Read Genesis 1:26-27

6. Does God base your self-worth on your past or deeds? If not, what can we learn from Psalms 139:13-16?

7. In order to have God's view on how you should view yourself (self-worthy), what needs to change? Read John 1: 12, Proverbs 23:3 and Romans 12:1-2

8. Having read the scriptures in this study lessons identify the lies you have believed about yourself and list five truths that God says about who you are.

    a.

    b.

    c.

    d.

    e.

Prayer Guidance

Pray that God will help you discern the lies you have believed about yourself and ask him for insight and understanding to know and embrace who He says you are.

Wise Choices Life Application

Lesson Ten

Discerning Deception

1. What is deception?

2. Discuss examples of deception

3. For a better understanding of how deception works read Joshua 9:1-27 and discuss the following:

   a. What was the intention of the Gibeonites in deceiving the Israelites?

   b. List the tactics the Gibeonites used to deceive Joshua and the Israelites.

c. If you were Joshua what steps would you have taken to avoid being deceived?

4. The devil often uses deception as a weapon to ensnare us, what can we learn from the following scriptures to help us discern his deceptive nature?

    a. 1 Peter 5:8

    b. 2 Corinthians 11:14

5. In order to discern deception what do we need to know? Read John 8:32

6. The most effective way to identify counterfeit bills is to carefully study the genuine bills. How will reading and studying God's word quip us in combating deception?

7. Since deception has a camouflage nature that makes it difficult to identify, what can we learn from King Uzziah about seeking counsel? Read 2 Chronicles 26:1-5

8. The apostle Paul gives this warning, 2 Corinthians 11:3 (NIV) *But I am afraid that just as Eve was deceived by the serpent's cunning, your minds may somehow be led astray from your sincere and pure devotion to Christ.* With this in mind,

a. Prayerfully seek to identify the signs of deception in the decisions you have made in the past or are currently facing.

b. Write down the specific steps you will take from now on to guard yourself from deception.

Prayer Guidance

Ask God to help you to guard constantly against deception and also to grant you the wisdom to discern deception.

Wise Choices Life Application

Lesson Eleven

Overcoming Toxic Relationships

1. In reference to chapter 7 identify and discuss signs of a toxic relationship in the following relationships.

   a. Parasitic relationships

   b. Insecure relationships

   c. Domineering relationships

   d. Manipulative relationships

e. Abusive relationships

f. Emotional relationships

2. Carefully review the discussed signs and identify toxic relationships in your life, this is the first step in dealing with toxic relationships.

3. The next step is disconnecting from those toxic relationships. Discuss how the following three steps will help.

a. Setting boundaries - Review Chapter 3, page 47

b. Accountability – Review Chapter 2 page 36

c. Support   system   –   Read   Galatians   6:2,   2
    Corinthians 13:11,

4. What specific things will you do to guard yourself
    against toxic relationships?

5. Disconnecting from an unhealthy relationship without connecting with healthy relationships only leads to isolation. Read Discuss the following:

   a. What are the qualities of a healthy relationship? Read Proverbs 18:24 (NKJV), Proverbs 17:17 (NKJV), Proverbs 12:26, Proverbs 27:6, 10, 1 Corinthians 13 & 1 Thessalonians 5:11.

   b. List specific steps you will take to build healthy relationships.

Prayer Guidance

Ask God to help you disconnect from toxic relationships and to guide you in finding healthy relationships in your life.

Wise Choices Life Application

Lesson Twelve

Embracing God's Plan

1. What kind of plans does God have for us? Read Jeremiah 29:11

2. Although God has wonderful plans for our lives, discuss reasons why we sometimes struggle to embrace His plans?

3. What lessons can we learn from the Israelites when they rejected God's plan of His Kingship over them? Read 1 Samuel 8:1-20

4. What are the blessings of following God's plans for us? Discuss - Review chapter 11, page 115 – 118

5. Following God's plans requires walking by faith; this may not always easy to do. What lessons can we learn from Abraham and Sarah when they chose the Ishmael option? Review Chapter 10, page 107 - 108

6. What can we learn about walking by faith from the following scriptures?
   a. Hebrews 11:1

b. Hebrews 11:6

c. Hebrews 11:17-19

d. Romans 10:17

7. List five practical steps you will take to embrace God's plans for your life.

Prayer Guidance
Ask God to help you have confidence in the wonderful plans He has for your life even when outward circumstances don't look favorable.

172

www.vesselofhonor.org

Inspirational Books

Becoming A Vessel of Honor

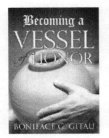

Today's Christian ministry arena places a great emphasis on developing dynamic ministries. Although having a dynamic ministry is important, training men and women who are after the heart of God is more significant. This book will challenge you to seek passionately a deeper relationship with God and teach you the way to become a vessel of honor and how to become effective in ministry.

Living Your Dreams

God has laid in each of us treasures that are intended to make us accomplish God's purpose for our lives. The secret to maximizing your potential, is unlocking the treasures within you. This book provides you with the keys you need to unlock that potential.

The Power of Vision

This book is filled with thoughts of wisdom and insight that will challenge you to look at your vision in life from a totally different perspective. Reading this book will equip you will the knowledge and motivation needed to navigate through the obstacles that keep you from pursuing your vision in life.

174

Making Wise Choices Seminars

We are dedicated about teaching biblical principles that lead to making wise choices in life. To conduct a Wise Choices seminar or workshop in your church or institution, please contact us using the address below.

VHIM
P.O. Box 24273
Cincinnati, OH 45224
information@vesselofhonor.org
www.vesselofhonor.org

References

Anderson, Neil. *The Bondage Breaker*. Eugene, Oregon: Harvest House Publishers, 2000.

Cloud, Dr. Henry. *Changes That Heal*. Grand Rapids, Michigan: Zondervan, 1992.

Dobson, Dr. James. *Emotions: Can You Trust Them?* Ventura, CA: Regal Books, 1980.

Gore, Nilesh. "The Rejection Is a Masked Deprivation." Article City: Free Articles for Reprint. http://www.articlecity.com/articles/parenting/article_28 7.shtml.

http://www.thefreedictionary.com/deception.

Neuman, Dr. Gary. "Dr. Gary Neuman's 4 Types of Toxic People to Avoid." Anderson. http://www.andersoncooper.com/2012/02/13/dr-gary-neuman-4-types-of-toxic-people-to-avoid.

Meyer, Joyce. *Battlefield of the Mind*. New York. NY: Warner Faith Pub.,1995.

Nikitina, Arina. "5 Steps for Building Self-Confidence." Solve Your Problem. http://www.solveyourproblem.com/artman/publish/artic le_697.shtml.

Omartian, Stormie. *The Power Of A Praying Woman*. Eugene, Oregon: Harvest House Pub., 2002.

Osteen, Joel. *Becoming a Better You*. New York, NY: Free Press, 2008.

Osteen, Victoria. *Love Your Life*. New York, NY: Free Press, 2009.

Powers, Dr. Richard. *Pathways to Spiritual Understanding*. Tulsa, Oklahoma: Virgil Hensley Pub., 1997.

Seamands, A. David. *Healing Damaged Emotions*. Colorado Springs, CO: Chariot Victor Publishing, 1991.

The Amplified Bible. Grand Rapids, Michigan: Zondervan ,1987.

The Holy Bible: New King James Version. Nashville, Tennessee: Thomas Nelson, Inc., 1982.

The NIV Study Bible: New International Version. Grand Rapids, Michigan: Zondervan, 1995.

Ziglar, Zig. *Top Performance.* Old Tappan, NJ: Fleming H. Revell Co., 1985.

Made in the USA
Charleston, SC
11 November 2016